My Chicano story
by

Damian Chapa and Karina Schmitt

My Chicano Story

AUTHOR'S FOREWORD

This book is the commencement of the trilogy of My Chicano Life. I've separated my life up into three distinct periods. This book, the first in my trilogy, is about the foundation of my life, my background.

For all of you out there to thoroughly understand my history, it's important that you understand my roots. Because of that, I feel that it is necessary to give insight into my history and the foundation of my life first and foremost. It's like the construction of a brick and mortar house; you must start with the foundation and not the roof. By starting at the very beginning of my life, you will gain an understanding of how I became what I am today.

To some people, my personality and my career choice is strangely enough strongly connected with my paternal grandpa and grandma. They were the patriarch and matriarch in my life. In terms of identity, there was some confusion when my parents met. It was as if two different cultures were fused.

They came from two very different backgrounds; one was of Mexican-American descent and the other from the rural Appalachian Mountains. When they met, two different cultures were married which weren't ready for each other especially at that time.

To all my wonderful, loyal, creative, and inspiring friends, colleges, family members, business relations, and finally my lifelong supportive fans around the world I would like to sincerely say 'Thank you'! Without you none of it would not have been possible.

Damian Chapa

Table of Contents

ABOUT DAMIAN CHAPA

Damian Chapa has a life-long career as an actor, film director, and writer which he started in his late teenage years in New York City. He started out as a stand-in in Madonna's music video 'Papa Don't Preach'.

In his career, he has worked with numerous celebrities such as Edward James Olmos, Raul Julia, Maria Conchita Alonso, Maricela, Billy Bob Thornton, Benjamin Bratt, Steven Segal, Jean-Claude van Damme, Tommy Lee Jones, Gary Busy, and Victor Rivers as well as poet Jimmy Santiago Baca. He also worked with Martin Scorsesein *Pas de la Huerta.*

Damian became famous in his role as Miklo Velka in *Blood In Blood Out.* Since then his acting career includes movies such as *Under Siege, Street Fighter, Saints and Sinners,* and *Brando Unauthorized* (also director).

In 1998, he directed *Kill You Twice* with his ex-wife Species Star Natasha Henstridge which led to an extensive list of movies under his writing and direction such as, *El Padrino I* and *II, Bobby Fisher Live,* and as one of his latest productions *Father Rupert Mayer* the life story of a priest who preached against the Nazis.

Damian is one of the world's most controversial script writers and directors known. He dares to create movies that others would shy away from simply because they are either not politically correct or because we don't like to talk about certain ugly stories such as the statutory rape allegations that befell Roman Polanski. Damian Chapa wrote, directed, and acted in his controversial movie *Polanski Unauthorized* which caused a considerable amount of Hollywood discontentment. The late David Carradine wrote that *Polanski Unauthorized* was "a masterpiece". Damian received rebuke from the Hollywood elite for this movie but the fact of the matter remains that he had the courage to tell the story the way it is based on extensive research he had done.

Damian describes himself as "an artist who is focused on artistic expression rather than popular opinion". Poet and author Jimmy Santiago Baca said on November 12, 2014 about Damian Chapa:

> "Damian Chapa continues to surprise, amaze, and fill the reader within awe. Looking at such a handsome man, a brilliant actor, one would never suspect the deep channels of sorrow and tribulation such a spirit has traveled, overcome

and grown from! BRAVO!

- Jimmy"

ABOUT KARINA SCHMITT

Karina Schmitt grew up in Denmark and has lived most of her adult life in Italy and the United States. She holds a Bachelor of Arts in Spanish and Spanish American Studies and a Minor in English Studies from the University of Southern Denmark with a specialty in Personal Identity Construction related to Chicano Gangs. Her Bachelor thesis is available on Amazon and Barnes and Noble in Spanish and English. Using the movie *Blood In*

Blood Out as part of her empirical material along with third party anthropological studies, she discusses why some young men such as the character of Miklo Velka, who is the main character of the movie, chooses to join violent gangs.

While working on her bachelor thesis, Karina Schmitt interviewed Anthropologist Theodore Davidson, Poet Jimmy Santiago Baca and Actor Damian Chapa for her studies to support her thesis. Later, she became the editor and cowriter of Damian Chapa's first book *My Chicano Story*. Karina has helped bachelor students proof reading, correcting and editing their bachelor projects and other academic work and continues to offer her services to students and aspiring authors.

Karina Schmitt continues her writing, academic studies and research on Latin American studies at the University of Southern Denmark, and is currently working on a book about Mexican emigration to the United States in 1917.

CHAPTER ONE

The Cotton Picker

"Bam, bam, bam!" From a short distance, the popping of a gun sounds like an M60 machine gun blasting out. The sound makes you freeze instantaneously no matter how used you are to the sound of a gun being fired. It still makes you cringe and involuntarily shrug your shoulders. It's a natural reaction like the way your body reacts when you accidentally touch something that is burning hot.

My dad, who at the time was only five years old, was no stranger to the sound of guns being fired. I was still relatively young when he told me the story that you are about to hear today.

He was born in a little Mexican-American town called Robstown in the State of Texas, a two-hour drive north of the Mexican-American border coming from Brownsville. When I say it's little I mean that it's one of those places that's hardly noticeable on a map. Today, there are just about thirteen thousand people living in Robstown but back in the days, when my dad grew up there, Robstown was about half the size of what it is today.

Robstown is a little over a hundred years old and named after Robert Driscoll. Although Driscoll was a white man, you must understand that Robstown is by far a Mexican-American town as more than ninety percent of its population is Hispanic and originating from Mexico.

A considerable number of its inhabitants are still illegal immigrants from Mexico seeking a better living in the United States and dreaming of giving their children opportunities that were not available to them in their homeland. Between the legal immigrants, the illegals, and those that are rightfully Mexican-Americans – born and raised in the United States - the culture of Robstown is a heavy reflection of its people and their Mexican roots.

Despite its small size, Robstown is full stories that you could spend an almost endless amount of time talking about but for now I'm going to tell you about my dad's childhood and upbringing, which is based out of this unique, small town.

His cultural background plays a significant role in who I am and what I grew up to become. We are oftentimes a reflection of our parents whether we try to fight it or embrace it. Because of that, my dad's story growing up in Robstown is important to tell. To this day, I always look back on Robstown with fond memories. My father's story allows you to understand the world in which he lived in and a world which I to a certain extend identify with.

It's the world that formed my Chicano roots and which ultimately is the starting point of My Chicano Story. My dad's story starts with my grandparents Jesus and Juanita Chapa. It's because of their way of raising their children that my father became the man he was and that I became the man I am. They are the true Chicano roots of my family, my Chicano heritage.

Jesus and Juanita Chapa, my grandparents from Robstown, TX.

My dad was used to hear shotguns being fired before and was told about the weekend's *bailes*, which is the weekly Mexican dances that are very customary to our culture. It's a sign of our people having a wonderful time and for the most has nothing to do with violence. The bands played until their fingers bled for all the Mexican-American cotton pickers who had worked all week long for the *Gringo.*

Contrary to common belief the word *gringo* in and of itself is not meant pejoratively nor derogatorily. The word basically describes a non-Spanish speaking man typically from North America even though it originates hundreds of years ago from Spain. We called the white man *gringo* to culturally separate ourselves from white Americans, and even more so in Robstown because most its population even back then was of Mexican decent.

At the *bailes*, there was a feeling in the air, a sense of liberation from working the cotton fields in the hot, humid summers of Robstown. It was like an escape to go to the *bailes* and something that united our community in celebrating our cultural heritage.

Because of its geographical location, the summers are ridiculously hot. As soon as you walk out of an air-conditioned place you feel the heat hitting you in the face like a ton of bricks and especially if you're not used to these nearly oppressing elevated temperatures. It's different from the humid Southeast of the United States where you feel dampness causing you to feel sweaty immediately. The Southwest is drier but nonetheless a killer in the summertime. The winters are often mild and even cool. Regardless the time of year it was, the cotton pickers of Robstown came together on Saturdays to escape the long strenuous days where the scorching sun caused sweat to drip out of their every pore.

Las bailes were the places where my ancestors were able to get away from the demanding, harsh voices of their "hillbilly" overseer who ran most mills and businesses during the 1950's. Life for many Mexicans was hard but despite this fact they always found ways to celebrate it and so the story begins with my dad, Rico Chapa, and my grandpa Jesus Benavidez Chapa.

Grandpa Jesus

Grandpa Jesus had become a purely self-made financial success after years of hard labor in the cotton fields. Through blood, sweat and tears, he one day reached a point where he no longer had to pick cotton anymore. This was his liberation from the oppressive *gringo* but he was not alone. He had unconditional and unlimited support from my dear *abuela* Juanita Chapa. We always referred to my paternal grandmother using the Spanish title.

Juanita Chapa, *abuela,* was a dedicated and loving woman who stood by grandpa's side through thick and thin working hard alongside him in the cotton fields. In their marriage, they were a team, one that you seldom find in today's marriages. I wish that more people had the same set of values and commitment to one another today as my grandparents had. I'm sure there would be fewer divorces in the world if that were the case.

My grandparents worked focused and steadily which allowed them to save money eventually. Most other field workers spent their money as quickly as they made it but my grandparents had a vision, a goal from early on in their lives, to pull themselves out of the bondage of the *gringo* that kept most people down below the social level of white people.

To some people the word 'bondage' might seem like a strong word indicating a type of slavery. It was not slavery per se but you can argue that there was a certain level of servitude present in the working relationship between the Mexican-American cotton pickers and the white man.

Today we're too overly sensitive and too politically correct in America to want to use words such as 'bondage' or 'servitude'. Words such as 'slavery' makes most people think of black tobacco and cotton pickers but they forget for some reason the Mexican immigrants who worked their asses off just as hard as the black man did. The fact of the matter is that most Mexican-Americans, as well as black workers, were stuck working their asses off for the white man, the *gringo*, until they somehow had the ability to pull themselves out of this bondage. I am proud to say that my grandparents did just that!

Mexican cotton workers working the cotton fields of Texas

Regardless of the relationship between these two cultures, most people in Robstown worked very hard to improve themselves and create a better life for themselves and their families. There's a gross misconception that Mexicans often are lazy workers kicking back in the sun with their *sombrero* covering their faces while puffing cheap cigarettes. In fact, they are some of the hardest working peoples you will find whether they bust their asses in the cotton field, put in long and hard hours of King's Granery, like my aunt Lilly did for many years, or they're fruit pickers in California. You'll find hardworking Mexicans everywhere; from dishwashers to constructions workers, school teachers and even CEOs.

Mexicans are very hard workers but with a positive attitude you will find in few other cultures than the Latino culture. Life is never perfect for anyone and of course, despite the happy times at the *bailes,* there were people with problems in their lives just like there is today. However, back then the small amount of people who couldn't deal with what life threw at them didn't spend their hard-earned money on cocaine and heroin or designer drugs as is oftentimes the case today. In those days, they might have spent their hard-earned money on too much booze or maybe a little grass. Things were still relatively innocent in back then.

When a cotton picker worked in the field he had a choice. He would spend five days a week picking cotton and two days drinking to forget about the picking or, as it was in most cases, he would spend time with his family. Others such as my grandpa Jesus were of a completely different caliber. My grandpa worked hard. He made the suffering worthwhile by eventually spending his money on opening a little *tienda*, which is the Spanish word for 'store'.

My grandpa opened his *tienda* and pulled himself out of his servitude to the *gringo*. He raised the quality of life level for his family. My dad's nine brothers and sisters all worked at one time or another in the family *tienda*. Everyone around knew that the little "Chapa" store at the end of the road would be open from 7am to 9pm every day except Sunday, of course. Grandpa served his customers and the community.

Sunday was resting day and reserved for the Chapa family. It was the day when everyone got together to celebrate life and go to church. This day was devoted to family activities of any kind, whatever brought them together. Any reason for celebration was welcomed whether it was *quinciñeras, Cinco de Mayo, el Día de los Muertos,* or just getting together with everyone over a wonderful Mexican meal or TexMex fiesta with *tamales, arroz con frijoles, carne asado, pan dulce, flan* and much more.

The family fiestas were special and an incredible tradition that many to this day try to keep up. It's a very neat cultural thing that Mexicans do and it's wonderful because it brings people together. It's not about money. It's about family, friends, and the celebration of life.

My *abuela* was the glue of the family putting and keeping everyone together. She was an amazing woman and a devoted Christian. Every day, she walked to church come rain or shine. The daily two-mile walk made a profound impression on me and inspired me spiritually; to see someone like her staying dedicated to her faith all her life was amazing to me.

My dad was known as "Roly" or Rolando and then later "Rico". Sometimes they even called him *la pálica* which is a Chicano slang term that means parrot because he was a talker from day one. When he was six-years-old, he used to serve hamburgers to all the *gringo* business people that came to eat at the little *tienda*, which also had a restaurant attached to it. When rich, white ladies sat down to order, he felt like, "Who am I to serve these pale-skinned women with their French perfume who are spoiled by their rich husbands after making a fortune off all the *spics*[1] who worked for them in the fields".

---

[1] Spic is a contemptuous term used to put down a Spanish-speaking person from South American, the Caribbean, or

He thought to himself, "Who is Rolando?" To most in Robstown he was Roly which is short for Rolando. Later, most knew him as Rico. Rico felt that these were white people and that they ran everything, owned everything, and knew everything. They were college intellectuals and socially distanced from the Mexican-Americans in Robstown. He wanted to impress them with his new, polished shoes and used to walk proudly and self-confidently up to the tables pulling his little tie up with a swift hand to greet his customers. He was like Jesus Chapa, the grand owner of the Chapa *tienda* and so it was okay to act vibrant, confident, and perhaps even flamboyant. His machismo was part of who he was, and proudly so.

You may wonder from where he got that way of thinking. He was a handsome, little Mexican-American with the gift of gabbing. He was charismatic and could tell a story like no one else. His stories captivated his audience in an instant. No one knew where he got his jabbing gift from but

Central America and thus used pejoratively about Mexicans and Mexican-Americans as well.

trust me when I say that the man could talk his way out of everything. For nearly seventy years, he managed to talk his way out of trouble no matter what happened but there was one thing that he couldn't talk his way out of and that was where he had to sit in the school classroom.

In those days, it was customary that the Chicano students sat in the back of the classroom. No matter how gifted my dad was, he couldn't talk his way out of having to sit in the back of the classroom as if to deliberately indicate his racial inferiority to the white students. Although Mexicans were the majority in society, the ruling power was the whites. The racism wasn't thick but it was luring just under the surface. Perhaps his inferiority complex was partially from being placed in the back of the classroom as if he were a second-class citizen. Really, he had no reason to feel that way because he was handsome kid but at that age you see life differently. The way people perceive you affects you and it affects the way your personality develops.

He used to sit in the classroom staring mesmerized at the freckled girl in the front row. From time to time, she would glace back at him with her beautiful, sky-blue eyes making him think to himself, "Oh, my God! She's looking at me. She likes me. I know it." Because they were in school, she quickly had to look away again pretending that she was reading a book before anyone noticed that she had any kind of interest in a Chicano boy.

In those days, in segregated Texas, it was not allowed for a white girl to mingle with a Chicano boy. This is long before the civil rights movements of the 1960s. In the 1950s' Robstown, segregation and discrimination was very real. My dad was a kid then and later grew into becoming a young man. But now Rico was serving these strange, white and sometimes very pretentious people in his dad's store.

The name Chapa had been written on the front of the *tienda*, "Chapa's store". He was so proud of it because it was the only store on the street. The Chapa store was a relatively small convenience store flared with Mexican items. It sold the basic stuff but had piñatas and Mexican *sombreros* hanging. The colorful influence of the Mexican lifestyle made the Chapa store stand out as a unique place to do your shopping. Even though in terms of its size, which was almost like a hole in the wall, it served hamburgers to the locals and everybody loved coming there to kick back while grabbing one of Jesus Chapa's famous burger. Even the *gringos* came into grandpa Jesus' *tienda.* They acted all nice and friendly when they ordered one of grandpa's famous hamburgers.

"Hamburgers? Jim, I thought we came here to get some of that spicy food. I was looking forward to some hot TexMex food. You know the stuff with the little, spicy chilies in it?"

A white lady was talking to her husband. She came off ignorant with her phony smile glued to her face as if she had somehow misunderstood what Chapa's Store was about. Her face mostly resembled a giant question mark but to Rico it was unusual for a white woman to come off that ignorant.

"We only have hamburgers and cheeseburgers here, ma'am" Rico explained courteously. His thick, Spanish accent accentuated the cultural differences between them. They were from two different worlds even though they lived in the same town and probably only a few miles apart but the Chicano way of life and the white man's way of life were nonetheless worlds apart.

"But, ma'am, we've got the best hamburgers in town" Rico quickly added with a big smile using his best salesman's skills which later in life would prove to serve him very well.

Although they had come to enjoy rich, spicy Mexican food Rico, sold them on grandpa's famous and scrumptious burgers and took their orders. On the way to the kitchen with the order in his hand, Rico thought to himself, "These *gringos* never cared one bit to be kind to my cousins or any other Mexicans when they were busting their asses off cotton picking in the fields. Why do they feel the need to come here to our store and totally act as if everything is in perfect order?"

Rico dealt with the *gringos*. He took care for them regardless of their ignorance and not because of the way that the *gringos* acted in and out of the store. The money he was now making to support the Chapa family was not coming directly from the gringos. Eighty percent of his income was from his own people who lived in the neighborhood.

Rico walked over to the cook to give him the order. The cook was his older brother Johnny. Johnny never smiled. He had a serious demeanor, was thin practically skinny but believe me when I say that he could move his feet like a pro boxer as fast as the speed of light.

Many of the *Pachucos* knew the back side of his foot all too well. No one in their right mind wanted to fuck with Johnny Chapa. He never backed down from a fight. Johnny was relentless, fierce and feared.

The *Pachucos* were the old-school Hispanic subculture associated with the zoot suits and street gangs of the 1940s. They were very flamboyant in their appearance wearing high-waist, wide-legged, pegged pants and long coats with broad shoulder pads and fedora hats that were typically color coordinated with the rest of their attire. Oftentimes the zoot suits had long watch chain dangling from their waist pocket down to the knees and even below the knees only to come back up to the back pocket. It was a distinct appearance that was rooted in Mexican subculture but in Texas the word *pachuco* also indirectly meant 'punk' because of the gang association it carried with it. It's like the West Coast word *cholo* which in modern American usage that pertains to Mexican-American subculture. It's a West Coast thing and about the way they dress.

As Rico walked up to Johnny with the *gringa's* burger order, he stopped for a moment. He had a way of making you stop what you were doing to stare into his eyes. He made you wonder if what he was thinking was what you were thinking. Johnny would say, "*Chingao*, punk brother. Hurry up man, you're walking too slow."

Rico didn't even notice Johnny's remarks. His eyes were focused on the large breasts of the white girl who sat down next to her mother ready to order three hamburgers. Alex, a little Mexican-American who hardly spoke any English at all, was Rico's only friend. Rico walked right by almost tripping on the mop bucket Alex was using.

"Come on, *chingao, pachuco,*" which is a nickname used in Texas meaning 'punk'. The nickname is geographically bound to Texas Chicanos and not used by the Chicanos in Los Angeles.

"*Chingao,* Alex! What the hell, man? Put the bucket in the closet. I almost tripped."

"Well, I was using it to block the floor so people wouldn't slip on the wet floor," Alex said.

"Put up a sign with tape or something! *Chingao, man!*" Rico said.

Alex always showed respect for the one-year-older Rico. He became the closest brother Rico ever had. No matter what trouble Rico got into, Alex was there even at the dances. When they got older, Rico turned into a very charismatic man. All the beautiful, Mexican girls wanted to dance with him and every weekend there were people desperate to have fun. They would stroll around the dance floor smiling at all the *abuelitas* and mothers as well as the *abuelos* and band members.

But as in most dances I attended later in my teens, there was always a *macho* who wanted to cut someone. There was always a guy or two who wasn't happy with the dance or the *menudo*, the tacos, the beautiful music or the beautifully flower decorated tables or finally the sensual dresses that flowed from all the Latina beauties.

There was always one *pendejo*[2] who just had to draw blood. Alex, who was a short guy, used to carry a knife with him wherever he went without exceptions and when he pulled it out it was almost the same height as he was but believe me he knew how to use it. As kids, we heard all the stories of stabbings at the parties that Alex attended. Everybody knew Alex as the little guy you didn't

---

[2] Spanish slang for 'jackass' or 'motherfucker'.

want to fuck with or he would, as he said, "Cut your ass off!"

Rico got in trouble a lot because for some reason people were jealous of him. The envy came out in a strange way as they pulled their *navajas*[3] on him every now and then. Alex was always there in the crowd watching, watching his friend and big brother, the guy who always introduce him to the *bonitas*[4].

Jesus wasn't at home when all his children were gathered around the family table one night. Juanita was making their favorite *sopa de pollo,* a delicious Mexican chicken soup also called *Thalpeño.* She was also making the traditional Mexican dessert bread called *pan dulce* which is a type of sweet bread made with cinnamon that you eat as a snack or for breakfast. They're to die for, a real Mexican treat. Jesus could almost taste his wife's *sopa de pollo* but had to work overtime at the store when a humble illegal immigrant came up to him begging him to give her store credit.

---

[3] Spanish for 'knife'.
[4] Spanish for 'beautiful' here referring to the ladies.

"Señor Chapa," she pleaded. "I need to feed my kids."

"Please give me store credit. *Ayudame!*"

Juanita would get angry with Jesus because behind her back he gave credit to people with regularity, people who were in need. He was a generous man but perhaps his heart was too big at times. He was well-known to all the Mexicans for giving credit when needed. Later, many of those Mexicans became lawyers and doctors miraculously. They were hardworking, ambitious people who would stop at nothing until they were successful. Jesus was nothing like them. He was just an ex-cotton picker who worked harder than most people making a decent and respectable living for his family. To Jesus family was everything.

Jesus was taller than most Mexican-Americans. Some people attributed this to the Italian heritage that one of his great-grandfathers had in his blood. You could almost see it in his *tejano*[5] face which had a hint of Italian in the facial features. Albeit the

---

[5] Spanish for 'Texan'.

Italian heritage, there isn't much of a difference between Latinos and Italians anyway. Additionally, nobody in those days cared to research nor did they have the time for genealogy. They were too busy working their way out of the oppression they endured in Texas which at the time was quite discriminative in the pre-civil rights days.

Nevertheless, Jesus for some reason was highly regarded by some of the *gringos*. Maybe it was because of his demeanor. You could tell he was a man of integrity. He didn't smile much although that was not an indication that he wasn't happy. Jesus was very happy but he didn't feel the need to display his happiness openly. The need to distance oneself is a common machismo thing that boys are raised with from young age. Showing your emotions can, depending on the situation and who you are with, be interpreted as a feminine thing which is a negative trait in a man and therefore rejected. It's better to come off a little aloof and perhaps cold than too warm and feminine. It's a macho thing in other words.

What Rico and Jesus had in common was that they were both very charismatic and handsome. My father took after my grandpa in many respects. Not only was grandpa good-looking, almost stately, but he was also tall which was something he had in common with the *gringos*. Maybe that's the reason the *gringos* liked my grandpa and identified with him. His skin color nor his Mexican heritage were not social obstacles for him as much as it oftentimes was for most Mexican-Americans, particularly in the 1940s and 50s. Even the *gringo* sheriff liked him who was the so-called white power of Robstown. They never messed with his businesses. He was a man that everyone liked.

Nevertheless, there was an edge to him and a look in his eyes. You knew not to push him beyond the point of no return. It was a look that only few men have. It was ancient, almost like the Face of Moses coming down from the mountain after seeing something no one had ever seen. My grandpa Jesus had a fearless look to him. He did not fear anyone or anything. He was a Chapa and Chapas were known for being fearless. Maybe they had just a little too much courage.

CHAPTER TWO

La Pistola Compasiva

My dad was a remarkable story teller and used to tell me Chicano stories from when he was a kid and a young man in Texas. I loved listening to his tales. They were action-filled, dramatic, and funny with episodes that made me laugh. Some stories were more serious than others. Some were down right hilarious while others were sad. My dad might have exaggerated his tales or changed a thing here and there but they were nonetheless true stories. No matter what the story was about, I loved it and ate it all up.

My grandpa Jesus has always had a relatively weak and compassionate heart for people in need of his help and for those of lesser means than him, as I mentioned earlier. He was a good-hearted man. Jesus had a tough time rejecting someone if his help was needed. From time to time, his good-heartedness didn't please my grandma even though she was a kind, good Christian woman with no ill-intentions towards anyone.

Even though grandma Juanita was helpful, altruistic and kind hearted, she didn't approve with grandpa Jesus in respect to giving credit to their customers. She thought that he took unnecessary risks for the business and the family if the patron didn't pay.

One day a poor, Mexican lady came into the Chapa Store. She was dressed in typical 1950s, poor cotton picker clothes that had seen better days. Obviously, she was from one of the poorest social groups in Robstown. The way she carried herself and the way she dressed was evidence enough. Oftentimes, women wore ratty skirts and aprons but many of them wore their long, black hair beautifully allowing it to flow and look slightly messy.

It was common for the immigrant, female workers to put their hair in a bun to keep it out of their faces while working. When they were off from work they usually wore their hair hanging loose making many of them quite attractive. The physically demanding work and working ridiculously long hours in the cotton fields took a toll on all of them. Over the years their skin became increasingly leathery. Their hands, whether that of a woman or a man, were showing the physical wear and tear that was unavoidable because of hard labor.

Grandpa Jesus' *tienda* was situated on Main Street which back then was a plain, little street. Today, Robstown is still one of those tiny, throwback, Americana towns but in grandpa's days it was even more so as it barely had six thousand people.

The poor, Mexican illegal migrant approached him in a pleadingly. She begged him to in his heart consider helping her and her children. She begged him persistently to understand her and to show compassion. It was more a pleading than it was a question.

She began to sob as she explained her misery to him. Robstown was even smaller in population than it is today and since the family had been there for generations my grandpa knew practically everybody.

He knew she wasn't from Robstown and presumed she was one of the illegal immigrants that had managed to get to the United States in search for a better life than what they had endured in Mexico. Grandpa Jesus could identify with her. Long ago, his own family had come to America in search of better opportunities than they had in their own homeland.

The lady's eyes were filled with tears as she pleaded mainly in Spanish for him to help her. She wanted store credit but knowing Juanita's position on that Jesus hesitated.

"Please cash this check if you can't give me store credit," she implored him. She could hardly keep herself composed. Desperation was written in her face. Jesus tried to calm her but to no avail.

"*Por favor, Señor Chapa. Mi familia me espera en casa. No tenemos nada. Mis hijos tienen hambre pero mi esposo siempre está borracho*[6]." She persisted switching back and forth between Spanish

---

[6] "Please, Sir. My family is expecting me at home. We have nothing. My children are hungry but my husband is always drunk."

and English which is very common for Mexican-Americans to do. In fact, it's so common that you don't even notice that you're doing it. It just comes natural.

"*Lo siento, Señora.* The store is closed and I must go," Jesus said feeling sorry for the lady but at the same time he knew that his beloved wife and children were expecting him at home for dinner too.

"Please. Please, Señor Chapa. I beg you to cash this check. I have to feed my kids." The desperation and despair in her voice seemed genuine to grandpa who was usually very good at recognizing if someone was trying to pull one on him. But for some reason it was difficult for him this time. He couldn't reject her pleas. He couldn't ignore her misery. She continued to implore him appealing to his sympathy and compassion.

"It's in my husband's name. The check is in my husband's name. Please cash it. I can't cash it myself, Señor."

"I can't. *Lo siento muchísimo, Señora.* It's not yours," Jesus responded knowing very well that what she was asking him to do was to commit fraud but the woman was as persistent as ever and replied, "*Sí, yo lo sé pero* it's my children's. *Mi esposo* is a damned drunk. He spends it all on drinking. *Para él no le importa sus hijos para nada.* Señor, ¿don't they deserve to eat?" She inquired appealing once again to his Christian compassion. Jesus looked at her with hesitation as he took a deep, strenuous breath. He contemplated the consequences of cashing her husband's check. His good sense of justice told him not to cash the check. But he couldn't stand the thought of those poor children going to bed with their little bellies rumbling with hunger. Jesus cashed the check making it clear to her that it was an exception only.

Back at *la casita* Norma, Lilly, Jesse, Olga, who later died of a disease, Johnny, Kiki, Bobby, and Ricardo were home. Ricardo was the slender and attractive one. He was Mr. Casanova, a real womanizer who at the same time liked the sound of people's heads cracking. He was a complex composition of being on the one hand the stereotypical Latin Lover while on the other hand he enjoyed fighting. Later, his temper and proclivity for fighting earned him a reputation as "Mexican gangster" in Ohio where they moved to in the '80s.

My favorite uncle was Johnny. He had more guts than the most ferocious and courageous bullfighter in all the Western hemisphere. Uncle Johnny was the definition of macho which to any Mexican man is very important because without machismo you're just not a real man.

As a young kid, you quickly establish your role models. You learn masculinity from them simply by watching and doing. At the dinner table, was Kiki whose real name was Henry. Young Bobby Chapa was there as well. He later became a straight-laced pillar in the community of Columbus, Ohio. Bobby always tried to stay away from his brother Kiki who had gone to prison for his involvement as a "hitman" in the Leal Brothers' murder. Bobby was like Lilly who, unlike many TexMex Chicanos, was focused on white values, college, education and white society recognition. Later, he became Knight of Columbus, Ohio and has been greatly recognized for his work and contribution to the community.

In the early days, Bobby made quite an effort to try to distance himself from Johnny and Rico who were the known "gangsters". He was like a flower amid thorny weeds that could prick your skin and leave splinters under your skin as though he marked his territory on you. He was the antonym of his brothers and always tried hard to do the right thing and stay clear of trouble.

In many respects, Lilly and Bobby were very similar. She had an affinity for 'white ways'. Like Bobby, she also went to college. Although I like my aunt Lilly, she would irritate me endlessly with her constant nagging trying to get me to go back to school. In her funny Chicano accent, she used to nag on me saying things such as, "Damy, you gotta go back to school" or "Damy, when are going back to school? You can't do this stuff," as if her entire family came from well-established, old, white money. I thought she was a bit of a hypocrite because to me she was always trying to come off as if she were more than she really was when in fact our family were just like most people in Robstown. We came from cotton picking, poor, illegal Mexican immigrant parents but Lilly was always trying to keep up appearances.

My aunt Norma Chapa had enormous influence on my personal development. I always loved her like a mother. She was the warmest, most motherly, down-to-earth lady I think I've ever known. I have no trouble saying that she was the exact opposite of my own mother.

Aunt Norma, as well as my grandma Juanita, gave me what my mother couldn't. They showed me what a real loving mother is supposed to be like. Aunt Norma was always working hard while maintaining effortlessly a positive outlook on life. She made you feel at home immediately even if you were new to the family or just a friend. She was non-judgmental, caring, and loving to no end. She was like a mother to me and was always there when I needed her. She gave me the support and love I didn't get from my mom. Her happy demeanor and the high pitch sound of her voice was always positive and welcoming. Aunt Norma's cheerful voice could be heard even from outside the house and she had a natural talent for telling stories with enthusiasm, drama and excitement.

Aunt Norma's stories always made us laugh. She had that distinct Chicano tone in her voice. It's that high pitch, cheerful voice that emanates happiness when you walked in to the room. It's always genuinely optimistic. I learned story-telling from Aunt Norma, amongst others. She showed me how to make a story come alive by putting soul into it. She taught me how to capture your audience.

They were all young then. All the Latino boys were protective of the girls in their family. In fact, the way they acted was like how some of the characters in the Godfather films behaved. When I refer to them as acting like godfathers around the women in the family, by that I mean in terms of being protective and demanding that others respect them. But make no mistake, they were womanizers. It pretty much ran in the family for most of them.

I remember seeing the Godfather movies and thinking how much these actors reminded me of my dad's side of the family. The boys were always getting into trouble with the law. Our family history proves that consistently. There's never a dull moment in our family. There's always something going on with somebody.

The girls were always good, Catholic girls though. They were not the promiscuous type of Catholic school girls you think of in school uniforms who act as if they're so pristine while they're screwing around every chance they get. The Chapa girls were the exact opposite. They were good girls that any man should be honored to marry. The Chapa girls were well-protected by the Chapa boys and believe me you did not want to get caught walking down the street with one of the Chapa girls without permission from one of the males in the family. If you did, you would get your ass kicked so profoundly that they might as well have packaged you up and shipped your ass back to your own *barrio* with a 'Defective' label on your forehead.

The machismo in the Chapa boys was of a whole other level that most people can't understand in its entirety. It's something so deeply rooted in the Latino man that it's not just something you opt to be. It's just plain natural to act in a specific way. Being macho is not like when you suddenly decide to quit smoking. That's a conscious choice you make. Being macho is much more profound. It's like your belief in God.

You see the mixed ethnic composition of our family particularly in their facial features. Kiki was the oldest one. He had a very Indian look in his eyes. Some of the boys looked darker while others were a little lighter skinned because of the Italian heritage.

Our Italian blood goes back to the 16th hundred when the first Chapas came to Mexico. Our name changed to Chapa from the Italian last name Schiappapietra. The early settlers of our family made the change after they arrived to Mexico. Apparently, it was too hard for the Mexicans to pronounce the Italian name. Regardless of the

Chapa family's Italian heritage, they were always and forever very Mexican. At least those on my dad's side of the family were very Mexican. There are some in my family who feels more Italian than Mexican which to me is odd because the Schiappapietras came to Mexico approximately four hundred years ago, and let's face it, a lot has happened since the Renaissance. There is a much stronger connection with the Mexican heritage than there is with the Italian. Perhaps it's just pretense. I don't know. But I'm not going to get into that here.

The important thing to relay here is that Kike was always very polite even though he walked around with a look in his eye that emulated grandpa Jesus' presence, like Moses just coming down the hill after speaking to God. You did not want to mess with this tough TexMex Chapa guy. He was very concise in his responses. I always admired him. He was a man of very few words but a lot of action. He was very manly in the Latin sense. Later, we learned there was far too much action going on with Kiki.

But there they were sitting at the table. Grandpa Jesus came in tired and hungry. No one ever disrespected grandpa Jesus. He was a real dad in terms of integrity, kindness, dependability, and love for his family. He wasn't like these punks today who coerce their women to abort their children or those who neglect to take care of their responsibilities.

Jesus slaved day and night to feed his family and build a better life. But no matter how much he improved his family's lifestyle and economic situation he never lost sight of who he was and where he came from. I heard stories of how he still remembered the days when he had to massage his own hands from the pain of picking far too much cotton for the *gringos*.

Juanita walked him over to the table, sat him down and began a very traditional way of taking care of her husband. She was everything to him and he was everything to her. They fused like two halves becoming one. Together they proudly raised their nine children. They always hoped that all their children would end up like Bobby. He was self-educated and ambitious. He always stayed on the right side of the law. Lilly was a highly intelligent, law-abiding citizen as well. She and Bobby never had a fall out with the law. They were perfectionists when it came to taking care of their taxes and never allowed any misquotes. They viewed the world from the authoritative and governmental perspective similar to that of the upper, white societal classes. They always had high regard for the government and the law.

Sitting at the family dinner table, Jesus smiled and looked at his family. It was only year ago, that he couldn't even buy a truck. Now he was full of well-deserved pride for what he had achieved. Jesus reminisced the past, particularly a moment in his youth when he had look through the window wondering if he would ever be able to own him own home. He had wondered if one day he would be able to stop having to pick cotton. Would the day come when he would be free from the shackles of strenuous labor? After all, it was people like him that made America rich, the entrepreneurs. Without America's entrepreneurs, there would be no manufacturing, no progress, and no prosperity.

As he sat with his lovely family gathered around the table awaiting Tía Juanita's *sopa de pollo* and *pan dulce,* he realized that he was part of the American dream. He could proudly say that he had done it, and he had done it his way! All of this had derived from the fruit of his own hard labor. He deserved more than what life had given him so far.

From now on, his goal was to ensure his family's continued success and prosperity. Never would he let the Chapa family fall prey to the *gringo's* exploitation. All his children were here in his own home and he was so proud of that but he had too much dignity to show his pride. Jesus wouldn't display his pride with a big, fat smile on face like some overly pompous and narcissistic *gringo* but his eyes never lied. He was happy to see them all together doing well and above all happy.

On this great family evening enjoying Juanita's homemade meal, he would never have guessed that half of the boys in this room would end up in prison while the other half would be celebrated in their community.

Rico picked up the ladle from the *sopa de pollo* pot and poured some for Jesus.

"Thank you, *mijo*," Jesus said as he took in the aroma of the soup Juanita had prepared.

"Papa, *oye*. There was this white lady today that was at the store today. She was asking for you. She wanted to know if you made your appointment," Rico informed his father alluding to the fact that Jesus ought to make an appointment.

"Ay, *¡mierda! Médicos malditos. No me gustan*," Jesús cursed in Spanish and continued, *"Yo no necesito un médico ¡me entiendes! Estoy bien. ¡Comamos, mijo!"*[7].

Johnny was always close to Rico but at this moment he was prodding him with a smirk in his eyes as he began to mess with Rico.

---

[7] Ay, Damn! Damn doctors. I don't like them", "I don't need no doctor, you understand me? I'm fine. Let's eat, son."

"Hey man, leave dad alone, he's tired. Anyhow, why you always got that twinkle in your eye every time you talk about that white lady?"

Rico, who was embarrassed by Johnny's remark, cursed back saying, "Dammit, leave me alone Johnny! Come on out in the backyard and I'll show you!"

Jesus was getting angry.

"Shut the hell up, you two and go to your rooms! All of you! I don't want to hear this!" he yelled.

Norma noticed how Rico was trying to act smooth and *suave* around the ladies so she mocked him openly in front of everyone.

"Rolando is in love with that older, white lady who comes in your store, daddy," she exclaimed. No one had a chance to comment or tease him because suddenly the whole table grew silent by a knocking on the door.

Jesus looked at Juanita. Juanita looked at Lilly. Rico looked at Johnny as if hell was about to break lose. Johnny was like a tiger and everyone knew better than to mess with him. "Johnny, get the door," they all exclaimed simultaneously.

As I said earlier, Robstown is a small town but back when my dad was young and still living with his parents Robstown was even smaller. With only five or six thousand people living there, it was rare for someone to come knocking on the door without giving notice in advanced. It was also the way that this person knocked that alerted everyone. The knocking had an undertone of an unwanted stranger's determination.

Everyone at the table knew it was a stranger because only a stranger knocks on the door in the middle of dinner time unannounced. It's one of those moments where for a split second every single person present looks at each other without saying a word but everybody is having the exact same thought, "Who the hell is that?"

Jesus slowly but purposefully turned his attention toward his oldest son Kiki.

"*Mijo*, answer it," he demanded.

Kike got up straight away obeying his father's order without questioning him. He went to the door while everybody else remained seated in anticipation. Everyone wanted to find out who was on the other side.

"Who is it?" Kiki asked through the door. No one answered.

Jesus had been around for a long time. He was a veteran in Robstown, Texas. Instinctively he knew at that very moment as if he could feel it in his gut that something was wrong, very wrong. His demeanor transformed from calm and composed to protection mode. Suddenly he was on high alert like a soldier sensing danger ahead. This wasn't a typical American family. It was a Mexican-American family and a family that partially descends from the Aztecs and Mayans.

The sixth sense that something is wrong and you need to be on alert is in your blood. It's your protective instincts as a man that sets in because you've learned it little by little from early childhood. It has always been part of our culture especially when it comes to the protection of the Mexican youth.

"Juanita, you and Bobby take the girls in the other room and both of you keep them away from here!" Jesus screamed at the girls and his wife. Bobby was always the good guy in the family and was never the one to get into trouble with the law. Because of that grandpa Jesus knew he could trust Bobby to help his mother take care of the young ones and the other women.

Women didn't question their husbands or other patriarchs in their family. They were more submissive, obedient and feminine than they are today. Nowadays a woman might say, "I want to stay here. I can handle it. Don't fucking tell me what to do!"

In the old days, the dynamics between the sexes flowed more smoothly as both parties were more accepting to the division of male and female roles in the family. When my father was young, things were simpler. It was a more innocent time. Juanita knew her husband loved her and the girls and that he was only trying to protect them. It was the man's job to provide for his family not only in terms of financial aspects but also protection.

This is where the Latino man's sense of machismo comes into play. It is his duty, his obligation, to stand up and be strong, masculine, and courageous for those who are under his care. Because of the clear division of roles in the family, all the girls got up and went into the other room as Jesus had asked them to do. Lilly, who later became a feminist, kept her anger inside. She resented being ordered around. She probably asked herself, "Why can't I stay? Why? Because I'm a woman? Well, to hell with that! I want to stay! I'm not weak." Rregardless of how she felt, she knew better than to disobey her father. Instead, she internalized her anger and frustration and went with the other girls and her mother.

All this commotion took place in a matter of seconds. The thought still lingered in everyone's head as to who the mysterious person behind the door was. Who would just knock on the door and when asked to identify himself said nothing? They lived in a Mexican area. In fact, Robstown has always had a large Mexican population. Robstown was a place where you could easily get your head blown off for just looking in someone's direction unintentionally and somehow looking the wrong way at a person you did not know.

Most, however, reasoned it was for good reasons that things were the way they were. There were frequent stabbings. At the time, Robstown had a reputation of being a dangerous and violent town despite its small size. The paradox is that it was still very conservative in terms of ideology and culture. Indeed, more so than most cities were back then as well as today.

Jesus moved cautiously toward the door positioning himself defensively ready to confront the stranger. Johnny left the room for some reason. It was somewhat uncharacteristic of him to elude trouble. On the contrary, he usually confronted it like tiger.

"What the hell is going on? My bad-ass brother never leaves the action. No way!" Rico mumbled to himself. Johnny was known to fearlessly and confrontationally stand up to anyone.

"Fuck!" he thought as his mind raced to figure out what was up.

A flashback brought about memories. Johnny had been in Corpus Christi just a few weeks back when two tall and massive *tintos*[8] were drunk and laughing at him while calling him skinny. Johnny had gone over to the car after picking up a broken brick. He had hit it behind his back as he exchanged some severe looks with the two giant, black men. At first, he didn't say anything to them. You don't do that because it can be interpreted as a sign of inferiority. You want to position yourself as strong and fearless. Finally, one of the black men looked Johnny in the eyes.

"What the fuck ya doing near my wheels, man! What the fuck! Better get your ass on running!" the black man shouted.

---

[8] Pejorative Word for African-American men.

Johnny, who never smiled, seemed to crack a wily and plotting smile at the driver. As Rico had looked out of the window from the car, he had grabbed a glass cola bottle.

"Hey *tinto puto*! How fast can you pick cotton?"

The big, black man laughed.

"Man, I don't pick no mother-fucking cotton. I work on the rail road. And let me tell you something. You don't get your spic-ass away from my car I will run your skinny ass over!"

Johnny had kept his eyes locked on the big, black man.

"So, you don't pick cotton, huh?" Johnny stated in a challenging way as if to openly dare him to a duel.

"No motherfucker! I don't! Get the fuck away from my car!" he repeated only this time in a harsher way.

"Ok, I'm really sorry. Just thought I would give you some hospitality, some southern hospitality," Johnny carried on. Johnny knew they weren't Texas cotton pickers. The license plate revealed the vehicle was registered in Chicago, Illinois.

"I'm sorry. I'm sorry, *tintos*. I'm really sorry".

The black man continued to look at Johnny. He got out of the car and towered over Johnny.

"What you sorry for, Mexican?" he provoked.

For a moment, Johnny had glanced back at Rico who knew his brother well enough to know what came next. And then, as if it were his last breath, Johnny slammed the brick into the tall, black man's face!

"Ahhhh!" The black man exclaimed while he dropped to the ground immediately. His knees gave in while blood started spewing all over the white car. It was a mess. A real, bloody mess. The other black man got out of the car and he quickly ran up to Johnny punching him three times. Rico had never seen such courage before. He was dumbfounded by what he had just witnessed and knew that this moment would test his own courage. He had no choice but to live up to Johnny's boldness.

Rico quickly got out of the car as if his brother was taking an astronomical beating. He grabbed the broken glass bottle lying on the ground and slammed it directly into the black man's head. The black man dropped like a bag of sand to the ground. That was it. Rico and Johnny quickly jumped into the car and screeched out of there with the wheels spinning out of control.

Rico snapped out of his flashback and quickly returned to reality. Before him, what appeared likely to happen was more violence. He refocused his attention to the door wondering who was awaiting them there. Everybody wondered the same thing.

Jesus looked at Rico to confirm his position. He knew Rico was wasn't like the other boys. He was street smart, a fast speaker and quick to respond. He wasn't all talk either but a great fighter if needed be. He was unlike Bobby, who was book smart and who would be the senator of the family someday. Jesus had great hopes for Bobby and wanted to see him aspire to be a respectable citizen such as

Senator Jonathan Fitzgerald Kennedy who Jesus' favorite politician. Rico, on the contrary, was the street smart one who ended up in sales and bullshitted his way to a lot of things.

"Rico, take your brother back to the back of the house," demanded Jesus. Bobby had briefly sneaked out to see what was going on but Jesus wanted to protect his son. He wanted Bobby to help Juanita with the rest of them and stay out of trouble. Rico listened to his dad. Jesus gleamed with his unusual blue eyes at his Latino-looking son.

"Go now!" Jesus ordered in a whisper. Rico grabbed Bobby and sent him to the back of the house out of sight.

As soon as he was gone, Johnny came flying past everybody with his .45 caliber pistol. Rico had no intentions to miss this great action that was rapidly unfolding right there in their own home. The drama was as if it were taking out of 1950s Martin Scorsese directed action movie. He almost sprinted back to the kitchen door area.

"Don't even move," Rico yelled. Things were happening fast suddenly.

As Rico turned the corner, he could hear the two men arguing in Spanish. It was Jesus and a 35-year-old chubby and big-fisted illegal Mexican. The man was massive and visibly angry. He was swaying from side to side deliriously drunk. The stench of booze oozed from him. It was obvious that he had been drinking heavily prior to coming to Jesus' house.

Kiki didn't say a word. He just opened the kitchen drawer quietly so that the odorous man wouldn't notice what Kiki was doing. Pulling out a kitchen knife when you get an unwelcomed guess is the first reaction of many Chicanos. It's pure instinct. I don't care what the politically correct white wannabes say. That is just reality for many. When we sense trouble, we go for the knife in self-defense almost immediately.

There was Johnny with a 45-caliber hidden behind his back and Kiki with a not so hidden huge knife in his right hand. Rico eyes were wide open waiting for orders from his courageous dad.

"*¿Qué deseas?*[9]" Jesus simply asked in Spanish.

The man opened his dark eyes to the fullest staring at Jesus in a way that made him look like he just swallowed turpentine. They were intense. It's the kind of look you see on the faces of crack addicts nowadays, a look of almost paranoia only back in those days there was no crack, just beer, whisky, and tequila.

Jesus had been around many drunks in his life. He knew it was a tequila drunk. Tequila causes mania in some Mexicans and sometimes *gringos* too. It messes with your brain and your sense of reality is suddenly altered. Your sense of right and wrong has long gone out the window once the tequila sets in. It unlocks a slew of unknown worlds, some heard of and some unheard of.

The Mexican man stood there swaying. He stared at the Chapa family from a world of total and

---

[9] "What do you want?"

utter drunkenness. He feared nothing. On the contrary, his courage appeared to have intensified. Yes, that's what tequila also does to you too; it gives you a boosted sense of courage that for sure you don't have. At this point, you're drunk off your ass. It's insanely stupid of you to engage in a fight, particularly with sober people, but you do it anyway. You're bound to get the shit kicked out of you but you're too fucking drunk to realize this. All you can think of is, "I'm going to shoot this motherfucker!" Even though you most likely couldn't hit an elephant in the ass if it stood three feet away from you, you continue to provoke a fight.

The scene grew more intense but it had not developed into a battle yet.

Jesus remembered an incident of an angry migrant worker who found the *gringo* sheriff screwing his wife. Jesus recalled the migrant worker taking a knife out and stabbing himself fourteen times in the stomach, arms, and legs.

"I loved you! I loved you! I fucking loved you, you bitch!" he screamed out loud to his wife. The man never felt anything during his rant. The next day, in jail, I'm sure his feelings came back with vengeance. Miraculously he survived.

But there Jesus and the Chapa boys stood with an illegal drunk staring them down in their own home. It wasn't unusual to be illegal in Texas. Heck, Juanita was illegal and so was Jesus in fact. Most of the cotton pickers were illegals but that never stopped anyone. Only the children were Americans because they were born in the United States.

"I'm going to ask you one more time, what do you want?"

Jesus didn't scream nor curse. He was a man who put earnest effort into being a good role model for his children. He didn't want his children to see any of this. But it was happening. Suddenly the man pulled out a gun and pointed it at Jesus. Kiki acted with great courage immediately.

"Drop the damn gun, *pendejo,*" Johnny ordered him. He was hiding the gun no longer but pointed it right back at the man.

"You fucked my wife! My wife, you bastard!" the Mexican intruder exclaimed.

There was a silence. All Jesus was worried about was protecting his wife and daughters from hearing these hurtful insults. He was always the one who cared more for others than himself. Back then and even more so in a Latino house, it was about respect. If you couldn't maintain respect you had nothing. That's all people had to hold onto. Sometimes you didn't have food. Sometimes you couldn't even get a nice, cool lemonade in the scorching sun from the *gringo* bastard you picked cotton for. But one thing you could have, even if you worked hard all day, was your self-respect. It was a matter of mental survival and a source of motivation. It was about survival of the fittest, and more importantly, it was about courage and being a real man.

The moment you disrespect a Mexican, a Mexican-American, a Chicano, or Latino, or whatever you want to call us, you have cross the line. It's the beginning of the end for you. You can cry, yell or scream apologies from here to the Vatican City while pleading for mercy on your bloody knees and it's not going to help you. This is the point of no return.

"This bastard crossed the line," Jesus thought. What the hell was this tequila, ill-smelling piece of shit thinking accusing Jesus for cheating on his wife with another man's wife? That's just something you don't do. It's wrong on all levels and for this drunk to show up at his house accusing him of something he didn't do was unforgivable. On top of that, this *puto* was yelling accusation at him in front his family humiliating him.

"Hey, *cabron*! This is my house! My wife and children live here! Jesus rarely cursed, and the word *cabron* was a word that was used almost paternally like 'come on, you stupid goat head, get your shit together'.

74

Jesus acted protectively of his family. No one messed with him in his house. At this point, he knew that the Mexican intruder was the drunk husband of the lady he cashed the check for. There was no doubt in his mind the two situations were directly related. It was a perfect example of how nice guys finish last.

Jesus had out of the goodness of his heart cashed the check for the lady knowing that her kids had a tough childhood like what he and his kids had faced. He had envisioned humble, innocent faces lying hungry in the dark listening to their growling bellies as they were trying to go to sleep. He didn't want to cash the check in the first place and had objected with good reasons but the sad faces of those little, brown children caused him to feel guilty and he had gone against his better judgment.

The empty faces of the kids reminded him of his little brothers and sisters that he took care of as a young kid while his mother was suffering through long hours of cotton picking. He couldn't turn this lady away because he wouldn't have been able forgive himself. It wasn't a matter of being a hero rather it was the fact that he felt that he had to help them. He made a bad choice.

Here was this drunk getting mad at Jesus for a doing a good deed. Bobby popped his head out of the corner of the room drawn by his usual curiosity but when he realized what was happening, he soon concluded that this was by far a safe zone. He wisely retreated.

"Get your ass back in there, *cabron!*" Jesus yelled at Bobby who retreated to the back of the house immediately obeying his father's command.

"Papa, I'll call the police?" Johnny was enraged. Things were happening so fast now.

"Listen Sir, I don't know what you are saying. I did not nor would I ever do something with your wife. I have seen you in my store with your children buying *cajetas*[10] and other items. I've always treated you good, and your family good."

---

[10] Little, hard, syrup candies

"Chinga tu madre, cabron!"[11] Then the drunk Mexican looked up to the sky and continued to shout in Spanish howling like a hyena.

"Chinga tu madre, Señor Chapa!" he bellowed swinging the gun around like it was a toy.

Johnny pulled back the trigger of his gun. He didn't screw around and he wasn't a man to engage in long, wordy conversations. He was all action and not for one second afraid to put his money where his mouth is.

Rico knew his dad had it under control. Jesus was very good at staying level-headed and keep his composure even if he was thoroughly pissed off.

"Espera, hermano…" Rico started speaking softly breaking the deafening silence that in a peculiar way had spread itself amongst the men.

Suddenly there was glaringly, loud music coming from the neighbor's radio. It was a very famous *tejano* song everyone knew by Roberto Pulido. He was singing loudly as if to entertain the entire neighborhood. The neighbors obviously had

---

[11] "Fuck you".

no idea what was happening and probably all for the better too. Jesus looked towards the neighbor's window and couldn't believe what he saw. Kiki snickered.

"Johnny lost it. Drop the fucking pistol, *pendejo!* Drop your fucking *pistol, güey*[12]!"

A very fat Chicana looked through the shower window of the house next door. She opened her eyes widely and screamed, *Aye, Dios Mio!"*

At that moment to everyone's surprise, Rico came around and quickly pulled the gun away from the drunk man's hand. He ran fast towards them.

"¡Tengo la pistola! ¡Ya la tengo[13]*!"*

Although Rico was not known to be a chicken, no one could have imagined that he, *la pálica*, would have had the balls to make that move. But he was born a Chapa and that hot blood would show sooner or later. Rico then gave the pistol to Kike who put it in his pocket.

---

[12] Güey is used in Mexican Spanish often misspelled as wey or guey. It's pronounced like 'way' and means something similar to 'dude'. Although used most commonly for males it can be used for females as well.
[13] "I got the gun. I got it!"

"I did it, papa. I did it!" Rico was smiling from ear to hear practically jumping up and down with joy and pride.

"I did it, papa!" he repeated as if he was astonished by his own courage and machismo. This sure was a big moment for him.

"Sí, mijo. You did it. Now go home, Sir. I am sorry you had a bad day. Go home to your family," Jesus said turning his attention again to the drunk.

The drunk swayed and could barely stand up. Then he suddenly belched. Everyone was so disgusted. Even the lady in the window who was now watching as if it were a gossip talk show felt sick to her stomach. Jesus took the gun that Johnny had and un-cocked it. Everything seemed fine until suddenly the Mexican man pulled a knife from his back and wore the scariest facial expression known to man.

"You cashed my fucking check, you bastard. Your wife is a fucking *puta*[14]!"

---

[14] "whore".

That was the straw that broke the camel's back for Jesus. After all, he was a Chapa. Something inside a Chapa's brain didn't give much thought to life's consequences. They always lived in the moment and never worried about what would happen an hour from now or a week from now. Everyone lived in the present. The disrespect was the present. All sounds around him instantaneously faded away to buzzing sounds and mumbles like the distorted sounds you hear sometimes while so thoroughly stoned that the world around you seem to have disappeared into oblivion. All he could hear was this filthy, drunk fucking bastard talking about Juanita Chapa. Juanita Chapa, the lady who gave Jesus Chapa nine beautiful children. Although one, dear Olga, had died from kidney disease. She was so though. Sweet Olga.

"If I die today I will die with honor. Maybe I will see my Olga," Jesus thought to himself.

Chapas were morbid in that way. Always talking about death. Death was always near. They treated it as a friend. No, not a friend but a necessary acquaintance. Something close to you so you would not be so fearful when it really stood in front of your face claiming you either to The Land of The Remembered or to The Land of The Forgotten depending on whether you were a good or a bad person.

"No," he thought to himself. "No one talks about the mother of my children like that. It can't happen. I am Jesus Chapa. If this happens and people hear about it, I will be disrespected for the rest of my life. I am Mexican. I am the blood of the blood of my parents. Of the Chapas. I am not going to allow this to happen. I gave him a chance. I tried."

At that moment, the raved drunk lounged at Jesus with the knife raised in his hand. Jesus, although older, was strong and swift. He pumped five bullets into the man instantly killing him. The man fell into Jesus' arms. His blood began to slowly spill out onto Jesus' jeans. He fell flat on his nose. You could hear the cracking of his nose as it fell and broke on the blacktop. The gun was still smoking from being fired. The smell of the gunfire was very strong. Back then as bullets were not made the way they are today, they smelled. You could smell them from yards away. Jesus watched and all the Chapa boys watched waiting for orders from Jesus.

Jesus was vividly angry. You could see the veins popping out of his head. But he was a very religious man too. He and Juanita used to walk two miles to church almost every day. She used to bless me when I was a little boy. I felt that spiritual heat coming from her hands on my forehead when she touched me. There were times when I wondered if her touch was supernatural or divine.

Jesus leaned over and then crouched down over the man's dead body. To everyone's surprise Jesus touched the bloody man's head and began to say a goodbye prayer.

"Vaya con dios, cabron. Vaya con dios.¹⁵" Rico almost shed a tear not for the drunk but he was

---

¹⁵ "Go with God".

worried about his dad. Always so courageous. He took the gun from Jesus.

"Dad, don't worry I will say I did it. I shot him. Papa, don't worry nothing will happen to you."

Jesus looked at Rico in disbelief.

"Mijo, ¿qué? Are you crazy? Give me the gun! ¡Damelo! Give it to me! You're just a kid."

Hours later the sheriff and all his men cleaned up the mess. My Grandpa was in the back of the Sheriff's car. Johnny told me the story of what happened when the cops arrived. Jesus put the gun near the dead man's body and simply raised his hands up but not way up it was strange. It was hailing sign. His hands were strait up and he said something in Spanish that sounded like, 'Is there no help for a widow's son?'

I asked my Uncle Johnny what this meant and he said he that he had no idea. I don't think many do. But the strange thing was that Rico watched his dad, Jesus, exit out of the back of the old sheriff's car and the three *gringos* shook hands in a secretive way with one of the pillars of the community.

Next thing you know Jesus was walking towards the house. He wasn't going to answer any questions about what happened. He simply sat down in his old chair. Juanita knew what he was thinking. They were always in sync.

"Jesus, do you want me to warm up your soup?" She asked softly. He just smiled as he looked into her eyes and thought, 'I love you so much I will kill for you'.

CHAPTER THREE

Donna and Rico

I was born in Ohio to two very attractive and outgoing people. My father Rico (Rolando) Chapa of Robstown, Texas, was a very cool and intense guy. He was one of nine children who grew up with amazing parents. My dad was the son of parents who were illegal immigrants.

My mother, a very beautiful and eccentric girl, from Kentucky had a twang in her accent. She was born near the Appalachian Mountains. Because of the rural nature of the place in which she grew up some people would describe her as a hillbilly.

However, after extensive research into my mother's history, we have found out that she is from an ancient royal bloodline. We had heard rumors of this when we were children. A friend of my dad, Johnny Todd, used to watch us and tell us stories about ancient druids that came from Ireland and other places. Johnny was a strange fellow. He was sort of a preacher. We found out later that he was a real life witch from the ancient witchcraft family, the "Collins" family.

Johnny told me he used to see my mother give what they call the devil horns. Later, I found out it was a Satanic symbol with the hand towards me. I thought he was crazy and said that my mother was just a drunk. Johnny Todd, who used to babysit us as a favor to my dad, told me when I was a boy that the reasons why my mother had the old stained glass, the Hexagram, in the window. He said that it had nothing to do with the Hebrews whatsoever but that it is an ancient witchcraft or druid symbol used in conjuring demons. He also claimed that it is the oldest of the ancient mystery school symbols.

When I was young, this didn't mean much to me but the strange behavior of my mother and some of the members of my family would certainly allude to the fact that something was very strange in the family.

One day, when I was visiting my grandmother, I saw a book with an upside down pentagram on it. I pulled it out of the drawer. My grandmother took it from my hands and quickly put it back in the drawer.

"That ain't none of your business, Dame," she said.

Later, I realized after looking at the book again that my grandmother was a very powerful member of the free masonic group called the Eastern Stars.

But in any event, my mother was from the Appalachian Mountains which is one of the poorest sections of all North America. It's a predominately white population plagued by extreme poverty. The location is very isolated. In fact, I think that the Appalachian Mountains suffers from a harsher level of poverty than most crime-ridden ghettos in America.

The people are typically of European descent. After I did extensive research, I found out that the family came all the way from Wexford Ireland a long time ago. I found that they actually had connections to an ancient Merovingian bloodline. Johnny Todd, who is now dead, might have had more knowledge than we did of our own family.

Johnny told me when I was a kid that he found it quite interesting that all of my brothers' birthdays where on or near Halloween. I mean, it is a bit strange that my mother tried to make it happen on Halloween.

My mom used to say some of the strangest things when drinking. Some of it I won't even repeat in this book. I know one thing; it was not a once in a lifetime thing to see my mother slithering on the floor when she was drunk speaking in strange tongues. My dad used to follow her screaming exorcistic words. It might seem funny to some readers but to a little boy who had a great deal of trauma already that sight was damaging.

In any event, the Appalachian women are beautiful with fair complexion and northern European features but the problem is that due to the ridiculously high amount of Mountain Dew that many of them drink their dental hygiene is terrible and oftentimes they're missing teeth. You can conclude that they're gorgeous women if they keep their mouths shot because as soon as they open their mouths, you change your mind immediately.

My mom was an exception to that, however. She was an extremely beautiful woman throughout her life and contrary to the average she had pretty teeth. The people of the Appalachian Mountains are known to be heavy drinkers and Donna was no exception. She was already drinking at the early age of only ten but no matter how much some people put her down by calling her a hillbilly, my mother, Donna Jean Michaels, became a Chapa even though she despised my dad for fooling her into believing that he was Italian at first.

Donna would do anything to get out of her Granny's house. She resented having to live with her Granny because of where she was growing up. The Appalachian Mountains was in Donna's mind a place where people had no vision, they lacked aspirations to a better life, and failed to have dreams of tomorrow. Seen from Donna's perspective, the men of the Appalachian Mountains are abusive both physically and sexually. It's a dead-end place, a hole in the wall but she had no choice.

Rissi, Donna's mother, had to work long hours and was not a particularly warm mother but Granny on the other hand had a very warm and kind heart. She treated my mother with kindness and love which Donna didn't experience anywhere else. My grandmother, the Eastern Star, is a contrast to my dear Granny, Donna's mother, who became a Pentecostal Christian. She had a warm and kind heart. She treated my mother with kindness and love. Granny also had a deeply rooted history in Druidic ritual. However, her life changed completely after she became a Christian. She did not get along with her own daughter and I witnessed her trying to convert my mother repeatedly. It was to no avail. My mother continued to go back and forth from Kabbalah to Mormon rituals and religion.

Although Granny was a loving grandmother and kind to everyone, unfortunately she too suffered from alcoholism. However, she was very spiritual.

She would pray in tongues as she sat in the old rocking chair singing, *"Swing lo Sweet Chariot"* all the way up until the chariot took her home.

Sometimes Rissi left Donna as well as her son home alone vulnerable to abuse at the hands of her uncles, whom all were freemasons. It's very hard to learn this about your mother no matter how wonderful a mother she might or might not have been. It's devastating to learn that she had endured abuse and harshness in her early life.

In addition to the absence of Donna's mother in her life, her father wasn't around very much either so she suffered from parental neglect from both parents. To top it all, she felt unprotected and vulnerable when Granny left which happened frequently. The loneliness, that was a result of the abuse and the neglect, was just as bad for her. Perhaps it contributes to the explanation as to why she herself became a neglecting mother because in all fairness she didn't have a key role model in her own life growing up.

It's so sad to think of a young child who consoles herself with drinking and takes to the bottle at the immature age of only ten. She drank to dull the pain and to escape the harshness of life's realities.

My maternal grandmother was hardly what you could classify as a mother in the traditional, loving terms. She was sexually very free for her time and had several affairs with other men than my mother's father. One of these promiscuous and careless affairs led to having Donna's brother out of wedlock. Back then, it was quite shameful for a woman to have a child out of wedlock and particularly because she had been messing around with other men while married.

Naturally this caused huge issues for Donna's brother later in life when he found out one day that the man he had thought to be his father in fact was not his father at all. It caused him to feel paranoid and he became schizophrenic.

On top of this tragedy, on both sides of Donna's family there were freemasons who from time to time took advantage of her in their temple. This explains very well why she was as messed up in many ways as she was. The cold and solitary Appalachian Mountains were no consolation but merely added to her lonely existence. Donna was dying to escape the isolation and misery she felt in Kentucky household. Every day, her desire to get away from the abuse of her uncles when Granny was not around increased. She was willing to do anything to leave the Appalachian Mountains. To her it was mostly associated with something negative, void of emotion and care. She was prepared to hitch a ride or catch a bus, anything to get a chance to meet prince charming; perhaps a handsome, Italian man.

She seemed to be attracted to men with dark features. She fancied about being swept away by a man with dark hair and mesmerizing brown eyes. The fair featured boys she grew up around repulsed her. She wanted to be as far away from the Kentucky boys as possible. They never understood her anyway nor did they appreciate her artistic mind. Additionally, she always felt as if they were trying to take advantage of her because of her beauty. To top it all, the Kentucky boys couldn't dance worth a damn. Donna thought they were like dancing with a broken leg.

When Donna was twenty years old she moved to Kentucky from Ohio. Compared to Kentucky, Ohio was a downright upgrade for the young beauty. There were jazz bands, night clubs, radio stations that played modern, exciting, and morally forbidden music like Elvis Presley. The "King of Cool", the famous Dean Martin, with his effortless charisma and appealing self-esteem played on the radio for all youths and anyone else who had come to admire the new sounds of the 1950s.

In contrast to the boring Appalachian Mountains where the radio signal was faint, in fact almost non-existent, Kentucky was the hot spot. She had a major crush on the popular entertainer, Dean Martin, and like most girls of the 1950s she would jump up and down screaming with excitement when she heard his soothing, relaxing and crooning voice on the radio singing songs such as *That's Amore*, *Volare* or *Memories Are Made of This*.

He was tall, dark and handsome not to mention he was Italian which peaked her interest even more. Donna imagined how different her life would be if she were Italian surrounding herself with the beautiful Italian culture, spaghetti, and whirlwind of Mediterranean warm-blooded emotions. She was in dreamland when she listened to Dean Martin and imagined being swept off her feet, carried away and kissed in the moonlight by a dark and handsome man.

She always had some sort of escapism going on. She couldn't take her mind of the thought of making love with an Italian. The white, hillbilly Kentucky guys could never even begin to muster the passion an Italian man had in him. For whatever reason, she was of the illusion that Italian men where the ultimate lovers, the cream of the crop. She was convinced that this fantasy, this dream of a better life, would separate her from her depressing history in Kentucky and make her world a better place. Getting away from the ugliness that life up to this point had offered her was her unwavering goal. She needed to forget all those moonshine boys who only wanted to use her.

One evening Donna and her girlfriend Sue walked into a nightclub in Ohio. She looked around and saw a mix of hillbillies, Greek and Italian men. There were also the black men who played in the band playing songs of Elvis Presley, Jerry Lee Lewis and other 1950s rock 'n roll bands. In Kentucky, such a scene was unheard of.

Even though it had been almost a century since the abolition of slavery, segregation was still very alive in the south and Kentucky was no exception to the norm. In those days, the lynching of black people was not uncommon and racism was especially rampant in Donna's town of Paintsville, Kentucky.

Ohio was a more progressive state and was not as discriminative. That is not to say that discrimination did not occur in Ohio but compared to the toothless boondocks of Kentucky it was reduced considerably.

When John F. Kennedy gave speeches on live TV, the entire bar was focused on what the future President of the United States had to say. Even the owner of the bar was in awe of Kennedy when he appeared on the screen. Little did they know at the time that the man they were watching on TV were some day going to become president. Much less had they ever imagined that a decade later someone would cold-bloodedly assassinate him in public while he was riding in a convertible with his wife, Jackie Kennedy, in Dallas, Texas in 1963.

When Kennedy's speech was over and his charismatic persona left the TV set, it was time for the band to start playing again. They raised the roof. The excitement filled the bar and all the Italian and Greek men grabbed their dates and hit the dance floor. These were simpler times and everyone in the bar was having good ol' time.

Donna walked up to the bar and ordered Seagram's 7 with Coke. She didn't order just a single shot. At this stage in her life, she was already a seasoned drinker. She usually ordered a double shot. Sue ordered a beer and started to surveillance the dance floor for any hot 'commodities' of the night.

The night was still young and both ladies were in the mood for an enjoyable time. Both loved to party and to dance and both enjoyed checking out the night's repertoire of attractive prospects that they had fun discussing and giggling about. Suddenly, Sue fixed her eyes on a new face in the crowd and her curiosity was immediately peaked.

"Who's that handsome son of bitch?" Sue asked Donna inquisitively. From a distance, her eyes were locked on a very handsome Italian-looking man who appeared to be there with his friend. Where had he come from? Who was he? They just had to find out.

"I don't know," said Donna turning her attention in the same direction as Sue, "But you better stay away from him because he's mine! He's got to be Italian as handsome as he is."

Donna giggled and took another sip of her drink. She was mad for Italian men and found pretty much all of them very attractive. There was just something about them that she could not resist. They were entertaining and exotic with their black hair, brown eyes and dark complexion. They were the exact contrasts to the bumpkins she knew from back home, those whom she had been dying to get as far away from as possible.

Rico, my dad, was not a boy anymore. He was now a grown and handsome man at the age of twenty-one who was ready to take on the world. He had developed an affinity for sharp suits of different colors. His closet of suits was quite extensive already. Rico, who had been raised in Texas with cotton picking being the most common profession amongst Mexican-Americans, took every step he could possibly come up with to reject the plainness that the cotton-picking profession represented. He loved to show off flamboyantly when he finally had money and he loved to display his suits. He knew that people would notice him and he loved it.

In Rico's mind, a little extravaganza never hurt no one. Rather it made life much more interesting and fun. He loved to be seen and he particularly loved to be noticed by the ladies. He wanted the world to validate him and to recognize his achievements. Rico changed his mentality and the way he perceived himself about the same time when he was introduced to the furniture sales business.

It was a big shot, Jewish businessmen in Columbus, Ohio who taught him how to *schreibe* that he changed his life. My dad told me that *schreibe* is a slang word that means "to write deals". The term originates from German-Yiddish I'm told.

The Jewish New Yorkers he worked for loved Rico and his salesmanship. One of them saw Rico's great sales potentials and said "Hey, you gotta put this guy in a nice three-piece suit. He can sell!"

And Rico could sell furniture to any *mooch* that walked in the door with her scrawny toothless husband. Rico was a natural talent. He learned early on from the Jewish businessmen that to be a successful businessman you must work smart, stay focused on sales, get deals signed, and always be closing. You can never take 'no' for an answer. You must get each prospect to realize that they have a 'need' not just a 'want' for something. The 'want' everybody experiences but it is the 'need' that brings you to close the deal.

Rico's great looks and fast-talking only added to the equation. The businessmen often complimented Rico on his fashion saying things such as: "You're a young handsome man" or "You look good all dressed up in those clothes." All of this built Rico's self-confidence. The little boy who sat in the back of the class feeling like an outsider with an inferiority complex was long gone once Rico started *schreibing.* He had learned much from his sales mentors but the most important thing they taught him was that retail was far more superior to wholesale.

Whether doing business in retail or wholesale, Rico, though only marginally successful in his profession, still managed to look good dressing in the latest and most attractive attire he could muster.

No one knew that he had holes on the inside of his suits. He was a talented actor, a master of deception. He convinced people around him that he was successful. Never mind what the truth was. The key was to make people believe that he was successful. Nobody could see his flaws, not even the beautiful Donna. Rico was the greatest dancer in the world. In the 1950s, it was rock 'n roll that filled the dance floors with jitterbug dancers. You see the jolly good ol' times of that era in the movies such as *Grease* and that is exactly what you got in Columbus, Ohio.

He learned how to dance in Texas when he was very young. He knew how to move. Back then, all the Mexican guys who were not from Texas showed signs of jealousy when they saw Rico's smooth and energetic moves. Even the handsome Greek and Italian guys couldn't move like *la pálica*[16]. Rico moved so fast and so perfectly that you would have thought that he was a professional dancer. Without a doubt, he swept the ladies off their feet when he

---

[16] Slang for 'parrot'.

asked them out on the dance floor. No one could resist him.

Although Alex was always loyal to Rico, he couldn't help but to peek at Donna from time to time. He was fascinated with her pale, smooth skin. She had the face of a doll. It was so pale it almost lit up the night club. She was the Snow White of the bar at any given time. Even for a white person, she was exceptionally pale.

"He's a heck of dancer, no?" Alex asked Donna referring to Rico.

Donna could hardly understand Alex. His Mexican accent was so thick that it was almost incomprehensive. When he was drunk he sounded like the cartoon character. He sounded like a Mexican bandit in a 50's television show. She smiled and looked at him.

"What did you say?" she asked him. She tried to sharpen her hearing to cut through the music and noises of the people in the bar partying. Obviously, she didn't have a clue what he was saying.

Alex kept on as if he either didn't hear her question or as if he deliberately chose to overhear it.

"That guy over there with the dark, cool hair dancing?" Alex pointed towards Rico. "He's better than Fred Astaire. He can move, yes?" Donna laughed at Alex' comparison and his accent.

"Oh yeah, he sure can dance very well."

"What's your name?" he inquired perhaps more for Rico than for himself.

"Donna," she replied.

Sue noticed Donna was trying to cover up her own accent. Donna hated coming off an uneducated country girl from the Kentucky boondocks but it wasn't that easy to disguise the southern twang. It was obvious that she was trying to put up a front pretending she was like a big city girl. Later, she perfected her acting skills and could fool almost anyone with an adapted Italian accent so thick you could practically walk on it but at this stage in her life she still had a few things to learn about acting and imitating accents.

Despite that, she tried extremely hard to mask her hillbilly background and her insecurity caused by her humble life in the remote Appalachian Mountains. Sue saw through her pretense. She knew Donna very well. To Sue there was no hiding the bumpkin upbringing that was marked by moonshine, booze, and cigarettes from the age of ten.

Rico was still dancing and spinning when Alex walked Donna over to him. Rico was dancing with a Greek girl. Alex simply took the Greek girl by the hand and led her away from Rico. That was how Donna and Rico were introduced. Donna met Rico right on the dance floor. Alex left them alone and let things take its natural course.

Rico hadn't felt the wake of Donna's stare from afar so he was more than astonished when he first laid eyes on her. From the very moment that their eyes met, they were as if they were chained to each other. They were completely oblivious to the rest of the world. His heart began to beat faster. He felt a rush of excitement through his body almost like the adrenaline rush you feel as a young man when you push your new, shiny car almost to its max capacity racing down the deserted street to see just how fast it is. He had never seen someone so insanely beautiful before. Not even the *gringas* he used to see at Jesus' store in Robstown, whom he used to secretly admired from a distance, were comparable to the fair-skinned lady standing before him. A bucket of iced cold water splashed in his face could not have awoken him from this almost trance-like stage that he was in as his eyes were fixed on gorgeous Donna standing before him.

'This is it! This is the woman of my dreams. She is my life, my death, my love, my hate, my lust, my anger, my passion, my pain. She is everything,' he said to himself.

They began to move slowly to the rhythm of the music. They were too consumed with each other to even notice what was playing. She mesmerized him completely. His mind was locked on her immediately. They danced. She was so close to him yet still a world away. He wanted to pull her closer but he wasn't sure what the right thing to do was. Donna, who all her youth had been fascinated by Italian men, looked deep into his eyes.

"Are you Italian?" she asked him. The question seemed random but that is nonetheless the first thing she said.

Rico was a little surprised by her odd question and wasn't sure how he should answer it. For a moment, he felt speechless. Should he tell her the truth or should he let her hear what she obviously wanted to hear? He was very race conscious due to the racism he was accustomed to not only in The Lone Star State but also in Ohio. Racism was still very much alive in most places like a ghost reappearing its ugly head from time to time. It wasn't like the scary monster you fear as a kid, the kind that you think is hiding under your bed or in the closet. It was a monster that stared you right in the eyes, unwaveringly, anytime it had the opportunity to do so.

Donna couldn't take her eyes off Rico. He knew this was his time to shine. The moment was right and he moved closer to her taking in the scent of her beautiful body, examining her pale skin which glistened as if it were composed of smooth pearls. He wanted to be a part of that world. He wanted to escape the poverty-ridden life of a cotton picker.

The Jewish guys who Rico described as the 'big shots' had taught him a lot. He had improved his English because of working and socializing with them. He had learned how to take care of himself physically, how to choose the right clothes for the right occasion and determine what style was his style. In addition, they had taught him the fundamentals of being a salesman. They took him in and they made him one of their own. He loved these guys and they loved him.

Rico knew how to talk. He talked like a machine gun once he got started on his sales pitch. He was the born salesman and could sell crocodile shoes to an alligator, ice cream to an Eskimo, and sand to a Bedouin in the Sahara Desert. Nothing could stop him. He was invincible. It was a skill that he hoped would help him with the woman standing in front of him.

But suddenly he didn't feel quite as articulate as he normally did. His smooth salesman skills failed him momentarily. He felt the pressure of the moment, knowing he would never forgive himself if he let this opportunity slip away. Donna made it clear she was looking for an Italian. So, what does a salesman do? He gives the customer what she wants, only this time it wasn't a furniture customer but an astonishing beauty dancing with him that he just had to have come Hell or high water. Only a complete idiot would screw up this opportunity.

"Yes, I'm Italian," he heard himself lying to her and unable to prevent the untruths to come out. It just happened. It wasn't intentional. It was just a burning desire for her that let him to lie.

"I knew you were. I could tell by the way you dance like an Italian and your clothes are so fabulous. They're the most charming clothes I have ever seen in my life."

She bought into his story wanting desperately to believe that she had finally found what she was looking for. Donna was so desperate to realize her fantasy of finding a handsome and exotic Italian that she was willing to buy any story any handsome Italian looking man told her. She was fully capable of self-deception. Her young age might have had something to do with it too.

Sometimes self-deception is preferable to the truth as it makes our lives better. Self-deception is easier on us than having to deal with reality when reality is not what we are looking for. We fool ourselves. We learn that this form of escapism can function as our self-protection. Self-deception is our defense and our weapon.

That was Donna in a nutshell but Rico was different. His point wasn't to deceive Donna. He was merely trying to not lose the beauty standing in front of him. Rico knew he wasn't exactly telling her the truth when he said he was Italian. At the time, he had no idea what the consequences of this seemingly innocent lie would be and that it would haunt him. He knew not that it would follow them later in their lives together. He wasn't exactly from Italy. Only his heritage was Italian although that was several generations ago. Even though he had Italian blood somewhere far back, he was more Mexican *en su corazon*[17] than anything else. He was surprised that she couldn't tell he was Mexican. Was she really that blind to race, which in those days seemed impossible, or was she capable of such high level of self-deception just to be with an Italian that she could lie to herself about his ethnicity?

Surely, back in the 16th hundred the Chapas emigrated from Italy to Mexico but that was a long time ago. The Mexican blood was by far thicker than the Italian was. The Mexican identity and the Mexican culture was central to our family, however. He was raised by a Chicano cotton picker in Texas. He beat himself up in that moment for not feeling proud of his heritage but what kind of a fool would he had been to let this goddess walk away just because of ethnicity? He would have had to be a

---

[17] "in his heart"

real idiot to let such a seemingly little thing come between them. It would be better to just tell her a little, white lie, give her what she wanted, than to lose the opportunity.

But the dilemma tormented him. On the one hand, he wanted Donna so badly but on the other hand he was proud of who he was and where he had come from. After all, he came from Jesus Chapa who was respected by many in Robstown. He was a Chapa and he was proud of being a Chapa. The name not only rang well in his ear but also has strong connotations such as pride, Mexican heritage, family bond, and machismo.

I can attest to that strong feeling of pride that being a Chapa carries with it. It's *en mi corazón.*

Rico wanted to scream at her that he was Mexican but he didn't. They were dancing so closely together that he thought he could almost feel her heart beat. He was torn. He wanted her to know about all the dreams he had growing up as a kid. How he dreamed of a woman who looked just like she did with her red hair and pale skin. How he dreamed of her accompanying him to Mexican dances and accepting him fully for who he is.

He didn't want them to start out based on a lie. He wanted her to be as excited to enter his world as he was to enter hers.

"Could you teach me some Italian? My family never taught me the language from the old country" asked an old Italian guy who had overheard his conversation with Donna. But Rico just ignored him as he was too focused on Donna. The Italian man could see he made a mistake by coming over to talk to two people who were obviously experiencing love at first sight. He walked away. Donna was holding onto Rico as her feet became loose after having too many shots of whiskey. Rico remained enchanted by her light blue eyes. She looked like a movie star the way she dressed, with hot silk pants which accentuated her perfect figure. Donna looked up at the handsome, Italian man dancing with his arms wrapped around her so tightly as if he was never going to let her go,

"You are so damn handsome," she firmly stated as if no one in the world could dispute it.

All Rico could say was "Grazie." It was one of the few words he knew in Italian.

CHAPTER FOUR

George Cash's Furniture Barn

By the time I was 10 years old, my parents had moved to Columbus, Ohio. Before moving to Columbus, we lived in Dayton, Ohio. The neighborhood we lived in could only be described as low income, white neighborhood. Although the pictures you see of Columbus on a postcard are very nice with beautiful skylines, the ghetto and the low-income housing areas of this city are dumps. They are rough places for a kid to grow up in.

Things have changed in the impoverished neighborhoods of Columbus since I was a child but not for the better. My childhood was not filled with white-picket fenced suburban homes, landscaped yards with pools and outdoor barbeques. Grand scale Sunday fiestas were also not common to do as it was in the Chapa household of my grandfather. My mother wasn't Mexican and didn't grow up with the Mexican fiesta culture. She didn't grow up with the mentality that life is to be celebrated so to expect her to raise her kids that way would have been unrealistic.

Around this time, Rico opened his furniture business which he enthusiastically nicknamed 'George Cash Furniture Barn' after the late and famous Johnny Cash. Name recognition is important in business. Johnny Cash was very popular around this time and so the name association you got from the title of the business to that of a famous and popular persona would help his business my dad thought.

Rico used his experience from working with the Jewish businessmen. It laid the foundation for a successful business. He was one hell of a multi-talented businessman and could swiftly adapt to changes. He was an actor. He would put on an act that was adapted to whomever he was doing business with. Rico lived the roll he needed to play to make things happen. When he was around Jewish people, he acted Jewish and even adapted a Jewish accent. Whenever he was around Italians, he became Italian. The funny thing is that at the time he didn't know that he had Italian ancestry. Our family didn't realize this until several years later after I had spent the summer in Texas with my Mexican-American side of the family.

My dad acted Italian to the point that he acted like a Mafioso guy. I think I got my acting talent from both my dad and my mom. Both could put on 'the show' acting convincingly their part when they needed to. My dad could change persona at a wimp. It was second nature to him. He really was a natural. I used to watch him, observe his transformations. It's not like a multi-personality disorder but it's similar in a way and that's how it works with acting as well.

As an actor, you must be able to 'live the part' so to speak. You must convincingly become the person you're presenting and that is what my dad did in sales too as I do when I act.

He became who he needed to be. My dad changed persona again when he was around Mexicans. He suddenly became warm, loving, and kind. His most admirable personality was when he was Mexican because I saw how proud he was of what he had accomplished in life.

This is the Mexican pride that shines through. He never lost sight of where he came from. He knew that he wasn't born with a silver spoon in his mouth and he was never ashamed of where he came from contrary to Donna. The two of them completely contrasted each other in that respect. One loved his heritage and the other detested it.

He was magical in the sense that he could turn brass into gold, figuratively speaking, because his salesmanship was just so good. My dad never put himself first. He was a very unselfish father and loved to do things for his kids when he had the means to do so.

One day he came home and told us that we were all going to the race track Scioto. He had made a lot of money and when we got there he had hundreds of Dollars in his pockets. He gave each of us $200 which back then was a shit ton of money and we went crazy betting on horses. It was fun whether you knew what you were doing or you didn't have a clue. My older cousin was there too having a fun time with us. It was obvious my dad was enjoying life and loving the fact that he could reap the benefits of his demanding work. Here he was sitting like a king on his throne. He was proud and happy as could be smoking a big, fat Cuban cigar that he had gotten from one of his Jewish friends. He was in his slick suit and with a heavy Chicano accent he screamed at the horses as they flew by.

My dad was awesome at gambling. He was never a sore loser. Sometimes he would win the bet and sometimes he would lose but he never lost control of himself as some people do when they lose in gambling. He was always a my role model in that respect because he showed us that this is about having a great time and that it was about excitement.

Some people totally loose it when they lose a bet or lose money in business. They become outrageous assholes, sometimes even throwing things at other people. I've meet a few of those in my life and they're obnoxious to be around. My dad was the opposite of that. He lost with grace and won with honor. He had the ability to see the good in bad situations and he had the ability to change like a chameleon when things turned sour. He was like 'you get what you get and you don't get upset' to express it in very basic terms.

From time to time, we were poor as a church mouse having to twist and turn every penny to put food on the table. These were the rice and beans stages in our lives but my dad managed to make it seem normal and good.

My dad fully understood the difference between being poor and being broke as shit. It's a mental state; being poor is a long-term and near permanent thing which is extremely hard to get out of because you're mentally down too. It's not just the fact that you're penny pinching and trying desperately to figure out how to put food on the table again for the next meal for your kids. It's a mentally depressive state that you're in. It's also a state of mind that is extremely difficult to get out of. You have positioned yourself as poor, as a loser and until you change *your* perception of yourself you are just flat out stuck there.

On the contrary, if you're just plain old fucking broke, which undeniably sucks too, you're not mentally down the same way as you are when you're feeling poor. Mentally, being broke is a temporary thing and you know in your heart it's only a matter of time before things lighten up again. You're able to better see beyond the current situation and toward what is coming your way.

I might say we were poor but truth be told we were broke on and off. My dad was magical. Had it not been for him, we would have been severely screwed. We would be broke as can be and next thing you know he had miraculously turned our world around again. Once again, we could buy all the groceries in the world that we wanted. That is, mind you, until my mother had once again taken all my dad's hard-earned money and gone on one of her journeys. Her drinking problem never ceased until her body practically gave in on her late in life long after my parents divorced.

My mother took off abandoning her family and her kids for selfish reasons. It was all due to her lifelong, severe problem with alcoholism. She would snap and take all my dad's money leaving us behind as if we were nothing to her and she would take off on one of her journeys for months.

Although it left my dad momentarily depleted for money and hurt, he was always strong and remained focused on getting back on his feet. All that matter to him was supporting his children. He was a real man. He did what he needed to do and he always put his children first and strived to remain a good father at any cost.

I look up to him and have taken that with me in life as a father. My kids are my first priorities and I thank my dad for consistently teaching me this even if I at the time was unaware of the fact that this personality trait of his would become mine someday as well.

After dad lost his furniture business, he began to sell aluminum siding. He pulled J.B. and me out of school to teach us the art of selling. Our grades in school at the time were far from remarkable anyway so my dad thought that it made more sense for us to at least learn a trade to become self-sufficient. It was important to him that his boys learned how to make money so later they could support a family. He became known as the Tin Man after the movie The Wizard of Oz, a story I will tell you about later.

While he had his furniture business, dad's routine customer greeting was optimistic to say the least. "George Cash Furniture Barn. Come on down! We got cigars for grandpa! We got doormats for dad! We got free balloons for the kids! We got the best deals in town! Come on down today!" I heard my dad yelling those words while I watched cartoons on one of those old-school television sets. I'll never forget what a character my pop was. He used to sell his heart out with his Chicano accent in full force while at the same time acting like a good ol' boy from the country decked out in suits only a member of the Rat Pack would wear.

For those of you who aren't familiar with the Rat Pack, I can tell you briefly that it was a name that the public and the press used for a group of actors in the 1960s centered around Humphrey Bogart and it included celebrities such as Frank Sinatra, Sammy Davis Jr. and Dean Martin.

My dad's furniture business was successful for many years until the oil crisis hit America along with the Vietnam War's negative impact on the economy. But that wasn't the only reason my dad's business eventually failed.

When my mom was back from one of her journeys where she left us for months to serve her own selfish needs she didn't step up to the plate. She never stopped drinking nor did she clean up so that she could have helped dad with the family business to bring in more money.

Mind you, she wasn't ignorant to the value of money in any way. For the most, she stayed at home when she wasn't off on a journey. During these times, she mostly slept during the day while drinking at night.

I contribute my lack of accomplishments in school to her. She was never around to support us with our homework. She never read good night stories nor did she ever help or encourage us to read, write or do math. We were on our own. Mostly, she was too affected by the amount of alcohol she had consumed. All she did was try to sleep off the night before. If not that, then she was already working heavily on the next day's alcohol consumption and starting yet another day with a fogged mind.

Life with mom was not easy. She did not receive parental love herself so how could she ever give it? It's contrary in all aspects to the Mexican lifestyle and appreciation for life in general that my dad was brought up with.

My mom did have certain qualities and abilities, mind you. One of them was her ability to frivolously spend money as if it grew on trees. This is not an exaggeration. I'm not even being sarcastic. It's a fact. Spending money she had no problem with strangely enough. While passed out drunk, she used to lay in her beautiful bed surrounded by the antiques that my father's hard- earned money had bought her. She was a bit of an eccentric woman with a passion for expensive antiques which she filled the house with. It's amazing she even cared about antiques considering the foggy state of mind she pretty much always remained in throughout her life.

She also had other "qualities" that didn't jive well either with my dad. She was raised Pentecostal by Granny but at one point she decided to convert to Judaism and had some dealings as I said with the Mormons. I'm not sure exactly where that came from. My father was Catholic so it certainly wasn't inspired by his beliefs.

My mother became obsessed with the hexagram and put a giant, stained glass one in the middle of our window. It was a quite expensive one in fact. My dad often threatened to sell it when we didn't have any money and it was hard to put food on the table. He threatened to liquidate it for grocery money when she came back from one of her numerous journeys but he never did. His love for my mom prevented him from taking such drastic measures.

As I stated before based on Johnny Todd's information, when I was a young kid, he said that it was a hexagram and that people use it to put hexes on it. Later I thought that he might have been crazy. But after witnessing my mother and some of her family and later reading book of Alister Crowley, I found out that Johnny "Collins" Todd, the Ohio Man, was not far from the truth. In fact, I did research it and found out that Alister Crowley used to paint this hexagram on the floor during rituals from black magic and he would stand in the pentagram. It is the same one that was on my grandmother's Eastern Star book. A pentagram is an upside-down star, as I stated earlier.

I also found out later that in fact the ancient Hebrews never used this hexagram. In fact, it was introduced by Solomon during his many relationships with pagan wives. This sounds right to me since I know for a fact that the hexagram is used in witchcraft and anyone with any simple research skills can confirm this. My mother's hexagram resembled just that.

My mom was manipulative as well. As many women unfairly do, she used the female card. She used her beauty as a carrot in front of his eyes. She would try to 'dangle' her beauty, using it as a weapon, which prevented him emotionally from confronting her too harshly. He always somehow forgave her for leaving. I never understood why he stayed while I was young. It was an emotionally abusive relationship. It was toxic. It was pure venom in many ways. Self-destructive.

Now, as a grown man with an endless list of life experiences of all kinds including that of love, I understand how love can corrupt your common sense. Now I understand how this tainted love can destroy a person making you do almost anything to salvage what might still be left although it's self-destructive to presume that something wholesome or even beautiful can ever result from it.

I never liked that hexagram because in my mind it represented the destruction of a beautiful person, my mother, as it was just yet another attempt on her behalf to figure out how she was and remedy who she was not. I later found out looking in her library on a rare occasion and finding out that she had many books on witchcraft, Kabbalah and ancient mystery religions. When I was a kid, I associated the hexagram with her negative behaviors. I don't think she ever really found herself. I think she might have died still searching for the real Donna and for happiness. I know one thing. She had spiritual problems for sure. I cannot delve into the matter of her spiritual malady too deep in this book. The trauma and memory of those, which my father called 'possessions', are for another book.

When she died, she left me nothing. All her belongings had been left to her younger husband whom she married after divorcing my dad. Ironically enough, as much as I disliked the hexagram, she had left me only that on her deathbed. I don't know if she did it to irritate me or maybe Johnny "Collins" Todd was right. She knew damn well what she was doing secretively. In any event, I rejected my inheritance from her and passed it on to my brother. He still has the hexagram today.

The experiences I had during my childhood lead me to become a more sensitive kid. My parents loved the nightlife. Their whole life revolved around going to bars and clubs. Of course, when you put two attractive and charismatic people together you run the risk of two people becoming unstoppable party people which is exactly what happened to Donna and Rico.

It wasn't necessarily a marriage made in Heaven, nor Hell. It was just that both couldn't help but being drawn back to the bottle. You also can't be absolute in the passing of blame because ultimately it takes two to tango.

They married young and they were still very immature in terms of raising a family. Rico was 22 but Donna was only 20 years old when they got married. Their romance lasted for about three years.

It was blazing hot at first but then as it so often happens in marriages the flame burned out.

It's not always easy to point to one specific thing that causes the love between two people to slowly but steadily die. In fact, what most often happens is a series of negative events that are never fully resolved and thus the fading love between them is never rekindled.

But something happens that becomes the turning point and for some it becomes the point of no return. It too happened to Rico and Donna. Once they had reached the point of no return, what seemed like true love at first suddenly turned into pure resentment between them. They could never fully forgive and get past negative events.

Surely, it didn't help much that my mom was completely and utterly unwilling to leave the bottle behind. Her irrational behavior stemming from her drinking was reoccurring and in my dad's defense it's hard to continue to forgive the same reoccurring problem. It takes two to create a problem but it also takes two to solve it. Both must give a little to get but when one is consistently falling back on the same negative path that has numerous times caused significant issues both for them as partners in life but also for them as a family, eventually resolving the same problem and rekindling one's feelings for one another becomes virtually impossible. At some point, the painful divorce is the best solution for the couple as well as for their children. Sometimes it's just the preferred way to go.

My parents used to fight about every little thing it you can possibly imagine. It was like being placed inside a live episode of the TV show *The Honeymooners*. In *The Honeymooners,* the tension is brought to a boiling point between the once happily married couple over the most insignificant issues.

My parents were no different. In a way, it was mentally sadomasochistic. A better comparison might be the film *Blue Velvet* in terms of the emotional dynamics between them. I wanted so much to have had a mother, that later in life I used to hang a picture of Ingrid Bergman near me and convince myself that she was my mother. It was all just an imaginary world. Bergman had all the regal qualities that soothed me. Yet, in real life, my mother was more like Ingrid Bergman's daughter, Isabella. Well, at least her character in *Blue Velvet*. She was stunning, striking, sensual and insane. It would have been better had Alex brought the Italian girl over to Rico instead of my mom that night at the club so long ago.

Without question, it didn't take long for Donna to find out that Rico was Mexican and not Italian. She used it against him over and over. She knew how to hurt my dad by calling him a 'spic' whenever her system was flooded with alcohol.

Her drunkenness regularly took over her sense of right and wrong and when she got angry with him, which happen often, she used to scream out loud "You spic! You lied to me!"

As I said, it takes two to fight and my dad had very little tolerance for her outbursts, particularly when he had been drinking too. It was an evil circle that never seemed to stop. Whenever my mom assaulted him verbally calling him hateful and pejorative names, even in the presence of her kids, my dad would yell back angrily.

"Fuck you! I'm Mexican! Fuck you, hillbilly! Why don't you go have another bottle of whisky, you bitch! Go fuck another Italian at the club! Go ahead leave your kids for another six months! You fucking bitch. I'll kill you!" he screamed back at her.

The mental and verbal abuse of each other never stopped. This charade of hateful and hurtful remarks continued for years. It would go on late into the night while my younger brother J.B. and my sisters, Katrina and Cita, held each other out of fear. My brother J.B. was originally named after Jesus Chapa who had passed away at this point. J.B. changed his name to Jose Bernard. Although J.B. was named after Jesus, his life was quite different from that of Jesus'. My brother was plagued by his Mexican name. In Ohio, the name Jesus is pronounced like the religious figure and therefore made fun of. In Texas, everyone knows it is to be pronounced in

Spanish and it's therefore not subject to ridicule. Instead, my grandfather was proud of who he was and the name he had created for himself.

For my brother, growing up in Ohio and being subjected to discrimination and bullying because of his name made life very difficult. It caused him a lot of turmoil which ultimately caused him to change his legal name to Jacob Bernard Chapa and from there he became known and referred to as J.B.

J.B. always tried to fit into the white system while rejecting his Mexican 'gangster family'. In many ways, he was like my uncle Bobby in that he was always in pursuit of white values and white ways. My grandpa was J.B.'s contrast in that Jesus embraced his Mexican ways.

Today, I wonder what my grandpa would have thought of my dad choosing Donna who represented the exact opposite of any Mexican woman that grandpa Jesus would have wanted to see my dad with. I doubt he would have been thrilled about the endless, nightlong screaming matches that ensued between by parents repeatedly. It was so contrary to the loving, caring, well-raised, good Catholic Mexican girl that my grandparents would have wanted to see Rico marry.

Mexican women take pride in their long, thick, and beautiful black hair and their exotic complexion so for Rico to marry a pale-skinned redhead that on top of that made my dad's life Hell, even though Donna was undeniably beautiful, probably would have been mind-boggling to my grandpa. To my grandpa, Donna would have resembled one of those white, Texas women who in his eyes were inferior to Mexican women.

Jesus was a respected man of his community. Although he hated it, he was proud to be a cotton picker and he was proud to be Mexican. He valued hard work and was committed to waking up in the morning to take care of his nine children and to supporting his wonderful, Mexican wife. But J.B. was just a little awkward, white and skinny kid with blue eyes. He couldn't have been more removed from his Mexican heritage by the border. He was confined to the mundane life of Columbus, Ohio.

However, the northern U.S. was more accepting of other cultures, especially Latinos. That never stopped J.B.'s peers from bullying him because of his name though.

Racism was still deeply ingrained people even, in the northern states, and there were times when I heard my mother's side of the family making pejorative remarks about my dad. They were often racist slurs as soon as he walked out the door.

What everybody failed to realize is the effects that this kind of verbal abuse between parents has on children but also the racist remarks coming from other family members behind your parent's back. It affects you not only in childhood but also in your adolescent years and into adulthood. They acted as if we didn't exist or heard it or at least as if we were completely unaffected by the slander and the cursing that went on when in fact it's the exact opposite.

We heard my mom's side of the family say things such as, "How long are you going to stay with that spic, Donna?" or "You don't need that wetback. You can start your own business?" Donna didn't defend her husband as one would have expected of a wife, particularly one that was constantly drunk and incompetent of running her own business successfully.

She depended on my dad yet she treated him like dirt. Instead of defending him, she agreed with her family saying, "You're right. I'm free, white, and twenty-one." There was always a tendency amongst everybody on her side of the family to put the Mexican race down and make the white side of the family seem more attractive. Deep down, I think she resented my dad for being Mexican. But I think she might have resented him more for making her think he was Italian. She was so consumed with anything Italian it was borderline obsessive.

Not only did she, but also everybody else as well, failed to see the big picture of this whole scene and the effects of it from a broader perspective. Somehow in the process, they all forgot one important thing: us. I cannot fathom how because we were her own flesh and blood. Her and all her family were oblivious to the fact that my brother and my sisters and I were all mixed in terms of race. When they nagged on my dad calling him derogatory names and bad-mouthed him behind his back, they put us in the same category because we were his blood too.

He reacted with anger, and rightfully so. It was immature of her to verbally attack him the way she did. She was 34-years-old but acting like a child. When she married my father, she was old enough to make a conscious, mature decision about the man she agreed to love, honor, and cherish for the rest of her life and no one forced her to marry him. It was out of her own volition yet she would arrogantly praise herself as if she was above him. She did that even well into her sixties.

It was a love-hate relationship because regardless of what she said about him, or what anybody else said for that matter, she couldn't hide the fact that she was still in love with my 'wetback' dad. The highlight of her week was when my pops took her out to the nightclub down the street from our house. My siblings and I would sneak through a back alley and peak through the back of the bar where we were able to see mom and dad dancing to popular hits from the 60's. They were a perfect contrast to each other. My handsome, tanned Mexican dad and my delicate, beautiful, pale-skinned mother could have fun too. The music seemed to bring the best out of their personalities. It was the only time that we felt comfortable watching them together.

At home, it was a different story. There was never a moment of peace. Rico wished he would have married the beautiful flamenco dancer that he had met a long time ago. They shared the same culture and she would have taken much better care of him than my mom ever did so the regret of perhaps marrying the wrong woman was part of the issue on his behalf too.

The other woman, the Mexican flamenco dancer that he was in love with, was a young lady named Maria. She was a gorgeous dancer that he had met in Dayton, Ohio. He chose to go against his gut feeling and chose Donna because of a far-fetched fantasy he developed in his younger years.

Donna reminded him of the pale skinned women he used to see when he walked into Jesus' store during his youth. She was 'the-grass-is-greener-on-the-other-side'-woman but a dream that would bite Rico in the ass over and over.

Donna represented freedom from discrimination for him. Ironically, he got exactly that from her: racism. He felt like she was his ticket to paradise. She made him feel like he got upgraded from the back of the classroom to the front of the classroom. He wanted to distance himself from the poor background that was associated with being of a cotton picker. He desperately wanted to not identify himself with the cotton picker he used to be. He wanted it so desperately that he had been willing to go against his heart and not marry Maria.

It was an illusion that he would finally receive the gifts that the white privileged society brought with them. He was convinced that in marrying Donna he would no longer be known as Rolando the Cotton Picker or Rolando the Wetback. He hated being associated with that and wanted more than anything to feel socially and racially accepted. He felt he deserved acceptance. After all, he had worked so hard to become the most charismatic, persuasive, and most well-dressed man alive. He was convinced that all that arduous work would pay off when he married Donna, for better or for worse. What he obviously didn't realize until much later was that marrying Donna, and not Maria, was in many respects for the worse more than the better even if they did love each other too.

Donna subjected him to everything that he was trying to get away from. He was openly racially discriminated against by his own wife, a gross humiliation that you should never subject your spouse to. In a sense, his own wife emasculated him.

God's lessons can be extremely harsh at times. It's hard to imagine a worse punishment for choosing wrongly even though, now as a grown man, I know there are worse punishments than what my dad went through for going with the wrong woman. I am sure there is a reason for God's will and I'm sure I someday will come to realize the reason and understand the grander picture. And when that day comes He will shine his light on our way.

Donna's background caused her to have deep psychological problems but Rico chose to ignore them even though they were red flags right from the beginning.

Donna had been abused during her youth by family members. It left her with deep emotional scars that were unrepairable throughout her life. It caused her to feel deep resentment toward men in general. In her mind, the only way she could stop herself from getting hurt in the future was by striking with vengeance first. It was a defense mechanism that she used to try to protect herself from getting hurt. She used it as a shield. Although Rico might have wanted to marry the flamenco dancer Maria, he still loved Donna so much that he didn't care how much she embarrassed him in front of people with her childlike outbursts despite the discrimination and abuse that Donna subjected him to. To him, she was the most beautiful woman in the club.

Her beauty was unfortunate for my dad because it meant that every guy would try to get a piece of her, and frankly her exceedingly sensual vibe didn't help the situation one bit either. Her need to be validated and wanted caused her to make bad decisions throughout their life together. No matter how much he loved her it was never enough. Most women have a basic need to feel desired and validated but for Donna this basic human or female need was multiplied by a hundred. It meant that the need was so intense and so profound that she was unable to control it. She had to be validated by other men and not just my dad as if his validation of her wasn't real or deep enough.

It's understandable that the need is elevated based on her rough and traumatic childhood but my dad had a need for validation and appreciation too which she failed to comprehend or acknowledge in any way, shape, or form. Unfortunately, their desire to fill their emptiness caused a tremendous amount of emotional turmoil between them which greatly affected the mental health of me as well as my siblings.

There were rare moments when we watched our parents embrace each other. My dad would put on a disc of Freddy Fender, a Tejano singer who became popular after producing his hit song *Before the Next Teardrop Falls*. Something about this song brought a sense of pride to my dad's face. These were some of the only times when my parents were happy to be together. I recall a time when that song was playing and my mother said, "I love this song. I love your Latino passion. I don't want to be with any other man and I love you. You are my *Corazon*". It was a word she learned from Rico. Otherwise she didn't speak Spanish. I watched them dance and embrace each other and I remember I was hoping that this day would last forever and that the fighting would forever cease.

After listening to Tejano music, my pops would get nostalgic feelings and longed for his old home in Robstown, TX. Luckily for us kids, he made the best Mexican food in the world when he was feeling homesick. He used to talk about my Grandmother Juanita and how she used to cook delicious *tamales*. He would eat her *tamales* all summer long. Juanita made the most mouth-watering tacos along with the refreshing ice tea that kept dad cool during those sun-drenched, steaming hot-summer months in Texas.

From Juanita's cooking, my dad learned the important techniques needed to make the most kick-ass *menudo*. Oh, my God! I was so afraid of his soup.

"Papa, when are you going to make that soup? That *menudo* soup you talk about that grandma made," I used to ask my dad.

"Oh, *mijo*, *menudo* is nothing like it at all," he usually replied. I continue to beg him tirelessly.

"Really, Papa. When are you going to make it?"

My Mother, who was standing in the background, would put on some Mexican music. Suddenly, as if she had undergone magical transformation, she wanted to be surrounded by Mexican music and films. She developed a fascination for Mexican cinema and started to watch it obsessively. She literally flip-flopped. Mexican culture had won her over and she became practically fixated on its idiosyncrasies – at least for the moment. Italian culture and the dream she had of moving to Italy faded into the abyss. Now walking down the street with a handsome Mexican man like my dad was the ideal and something that in a wondrous way brought a smile to her face.

Out of the blue, my dad was her Mexican Elvis. He slicked his hair back and wore a suit that only he could pull off. My parents seemed to have found a new love for each other, a new spark that strengthened their bond. For almost two months they didn't touch a bottle of whiskey or tequila. They were temporarily transformed. They wanted to live and experience the bright side of life and it was at that point that I knew I was a part of them. I felt I connected with them somehow. It was a connection I hadn't felt before. I became hopeful of a more positive future where family life and family values would be central to our lives. But the dream was shattered when I realized it didn't last and I became disillusioned about the possibility of a happy and lasting marriage.

By then, I had reached the age of twelve when I began to form my half Mexican and half white identity. It was time to start soul searching and embrace who I truly am. My dad cooked *menudo* and I loved it. I was not afraid of it anymore. I would drench my food in hot sauce and savor it for days. I started taking mental notes when my dad spoke Spanish and I rehearsed my notes when I was alone in front of the mirror. I worried that if I spoke Spanish in front of my mother's side of the family they might call me a "spic". Regardless, I wanted to be just like my pops and speaking Spanish was just the beginning.

"Hey, I know you like *menudo* but now it's time for *tacos de cabeza,*" he said. My dad used to mix in Spanish with English. I didn't know what that meant.

"Don't worry. Just try them," he said.

"Papa, I know what *menudo* is. It's cow stomach and I know what tacos are but what is '*de cabeza*'? What did you call it daddy?"

Dad smiled to himself and walked out fast while yelling over his shoulder,

"You can't learn how to be a Chicano in one night, *mijo*! You're still my little, white chicken boy!" He laughed and continued, "I'm in a hurry. Gotta go to work now."

He had to sell tons of furniture to feed all five kids and sometimes business was slow as it is in most sales jobs.

"Wake up your mom. She's sleeping. Get her up," he shouted as he left running to get to work. I always heard him get in the car saying, "Donna *mañana*" because at this point she was drinking

every day and wouldn't do anything until 'mañana'.
For her, everything was tomorrow now.

CHAPTER FIVE

Seagram's 7 and the Country Girl

I don't remember the exact date but when I was about twelve years old I remember one day walking into my mother's room which was beautifully decorated with her collection of antiques. You could hear from the way she was breathing that she was in deep sleep. She had passed out from yet another night of heavy drinking.

As I observed her from a short distance, the phone rang suddenly. I really didn't want to answer. I felt angry and scared all at the same time. I wanted her to answer the phone but she wasn't moving at all. A war could have broken out right outside our door and nothing could have woken her up.

I was a different boy then, a different person than the man I am today. In fact, I was extremely shy at that age and the sound of the phone ringing made me nervous. Every time the phone rang I felt uneasy and I felt I was being put on the spot. I hated having to answer it only to realize it was yet another persistent bill collector who wanted to shut down our power supply.

I was still a kid and I really wasn't ready to deal with those kinds of responsibilities yet. They were realistically my parents' responsibilities. Nor did I want to be the one to relay the bad news to my parents. I felt caught in the middle of two evils. On the one side, I felt almost obligated to answer the phone because no one else were there to do it but on the other side I wanted my mom to step it up because I felt it was her job. It was her responsibility as an adult to do so. After all, she was the grown up in the house when my dad was working even though she didn't act like a responsible parent.

I smelled alcohol on my mother's breath. Although at the time I didn't give it much thought, I remember becoming dizzy from the stench of booze. I was so used to the smell of booze coming from her that I just expected that odor from her whenever I came near. The phone rang persistently for what seemed like forever until finally I picked it up.

"Hello," I said timidly.

"Hola. ¿Quién es?"

A sweet lady's voice sounded on the other end of the line asking who was answering the phone. I lucked out that day. Obviously, it was not someone from collections and I felt relieved. A heavy load was already taken off my shoulders by the sound of the voice on the other end of the line.

I was already picking up Spanish quite well at this stage from listening to my dad. Considering I was a twelve-year-old boy from Ohio where English without a doubt is the predominate language, my level of understanding was relatively good.

"Es Juanita Chapa?" I responded to the woman on the phone thinking it might be my grandmother. It turned out that it was my aunt Lilly.

"Who is this?" she asked with a heavy TexMex accent. I was so excited to hear who it was. Not just because it wasn't some bill collector calling again but because it was my family from Robstown, TX calling.

"This is Damian, Damian Chapa!" I replied eagerly. I couldn't believe it. This was great!

"Damy? Damy! This is *tu tía*, Lilly. I wanted to speak to your dad. Is he there?"

"*No, tía.* He is not here." I was excited to get the opportunity to make use of my Spanish vocabulary as much as I could. My Spanish was still very basic at this point. It was not until my time at my grandma's house in Texas that my knowledge of Spanish and my vocabulary expanded significantly.

"Oh *mijo*, you speak Spanish!" she remarked pleased to hear that her nephew had picked up her native tongue.

"*No tía*, I just remember my dad told me to say *tía* to all my aunts. I only know how to say *Donna mañana, tacos*, and *menudo*."

Lilly laughed and told my grandmother in Spanish, who was sitting right next to her, how I spoke a few words of Spanish. Grandma Juanita Chapa was laughing in the background joyfully at the good news about her grandson and I'll never forget how beautiful her laughter sounded. It was truly music in my ears. I never heard that kind of laughter from a woman in my own house. She was a true mother. She was a real mother who always sacrificed herself for her children. She was the epitome of a Mexican lady who had respect for herself and others and I knew she walked to church every day her entire life which to me said an awful lot about her character.

My mom never did any of that. Catholicism was never part of her life but it was a very significant part of my grandma Juanita's life. The two women were such a stark contrast to each other. I think it's fair to say that the two women were hardly comparable at all. I longed for a mother who would be there for her children, a mother who would genuinely laugh with her children, spend quality time with them and not just with the bottle.

"Damy, why don't you come down to visit us in Robstown this summer? *Mijo*, come on down. Me and grandma will cook for you. Do you like Mexican food, *mijo*?"

The invitation to come stay with my dad's family in Texas was irresistible. Why would I not want to do that? I loved dad's cooking so I jumped on the opportunity immediately. It was simply too good to pass up.

"I love Mexican food! I really do!"

Although I was a bit of a shy boy at the time, I was also an emotional and very sensitive boy which meant I couldn't hide my excitement. Whenever I felt sadness in my life, I couldn't hide it but at the same token whenever I felt happy or excited about something, I expressed it openly. I loved Mexican cooking which is so different in all aspects from the typical American cooking you find in the northeastern states. In my mind, it was a whole new world of amazing flavors combined in interesting, unimaginary ways. I couldn't get enough of those hot spices. They made my taste buds jump with joy and I can only attribute this to my Mexican genes. My dad introduced me to the Mexican cuisine and my love for *el picante sabor mexicano*[18] has never left me. It's part of my identity.

While still on the phone with *tía,* I ran back to my mom's room. She was dead asleep as expected still. I nearly yelled at her knowing just talking gently to her was a moot point.

"Mom, wake up!" I yelled at her.

On the phone, I could hear *tía's* happy voice.

"*Mijo,* you would love it down here." I looked around as I thought to myself, 'Yes, I would'.

I wouldn't have to listen to Donna and Rico fight anymore. I was already imagining how I would be able to feel relaxed and comforted in my grandmother's welcoming arms. At the other end of the line, *Tía's* voice was so calm and serene. I wanted nothing more than to jump on the first flight to Robstown. It could not happen fast enough. It was going to be amazing to spend the entire summer at my grandma's house in Texas far away from my mother's unstoppable drinking and my parent's screaming fits fighting over anything. This

---

[18] 'the spicy Mexican flavor'.

was like winning the lottery. How could a boy like me be lucky enough to be invited down to my grandma's house for an entire summer. I felt so fortunate.

Later that day, my dad came home late from work. My mother was visibly upset. She was still drunk even though she had practically been unconscious most of the day but her constant drinking hardly ever left her sober.

Immediately after my dad walked in the house, the fighting and name calling ensued again. I was incredibly sick and tired of all of it and I hated hearing them scream at each other. All the arguments were pointless and senseless. It was just rage and discontentment. Nothing was ever resolved. Nothing good ever came out of them. It was just an ongoing, unnerving negative vibe. It would have been better if they never talked to each other rather than the endless war of the Chapas.

At that moment, as at any other time when my parents picked up the fighting, I just wanted to run away from everything. Their uncontrolled outbursts were literally causing me to have painful stomach ulcers. All I wanted to do was to get a one-way ticket out of there to see my grandmother where I could feel safe. I felt as though her spirit was calling me. I imagined it to be a journey, one I would never forget. And the truth is, I never did forget my summer at grandma's house in Robstown.

The next morning, I woke up to the sound of dad's crying voice. He was all choked up and tears were running down his face.

"Dad, what's wrong?" I asked him worriedly.

"*Chinga puta! Chinga gringa! Chinga tu madre!*" He was screaming out the window.

Though I was confused at first as to what was going on, I quickly learned that my mother had taken all the money my dad had saved up, in fact over two thousand dollars. This was in the late 1970s and back then two thousand dollars was an awful lot of money. For many today, it still is a lot of money but considering the time it was devastating to him. He needed that money to pay the bills and he had planned to use what was left over to take his kids on a fishing trip. He was even going to cook *menudo* and *tacos de cabeza* for us.

"Daddy, it will be ok." I said trying to calm him down.

"*No. Tú no sabes nada, mijo, mi corazón.* Baby, papa loves you. Daddy loves you, *mijo*, you're my little chicken," he said.

Then he hugged the girls. All of us kids were crying. We were confused and scared as she had once again left us.

"We love you papa. We love you, don't worry." They cried back trying to console my dad's broken heart.

The thing that must be understood clearly here is that Donna was addicted to drama. Her life was like a roller coaster. She was never satisfied living a normal, mentally healthy life like everyone else. She was like a non-stop soap opera and she was never able to leave the booze behind. Donna was still chasing a fantasy world, constantly in search of her next fix like a drama-holic. All she ever wanted to do was to party and be free. I have heard her line a million times. I have heard it so often that it's sickening.

She always said, 'I'm free, white, and twenty-one'. She didn't realize it but the truth of the matter is sadly enough that she was all screwed up. When she had children, she never bothered to step it up to provide a normal and decent upbringing for them. It was all about satisfying her needs, her need for attention and validation.

You really can't call her a narcissist because she was not infatuated with herself. Rather, she was trying to escape who she really was. She had an immature kid in need of acceptance and validation. She sought it through partying and dancing. She needed to feel forever young, free, and careless. She could not handle normal responsibilities. She didn't want to be accountable for anything. There was nothing that could quench her thirst for the 'living on the edge lifestyle'. She had become accustomed to living in a dream world always seeing things from different perspectives than anyone else around her.

It's sad and terrible that even my dad's love and commitment to her was not enough to turn her around. Giving birth to five children was never enough to turn her around. She just kept running. In some respects, she was like the character named Kathrine played by the fair, British actress Lindsay Duncan in *Under the Tuscan Sun*.

My dad's Mexican blood and her bloodline created a group of children with a unique set of talents and abilities, but she never took a moment to sit back and realize the gifts, her children, that she was given and so because of that she took us for granted.

She failed to value and cherish the precious gift that children are to their parents. They are God-sent. All she cared about was getting smashed and reminding everyone that she was "free, white, and twenty-one." It was pitiful to no end. All my dad wanted to do was love her and be with her but his love was never enough for Donna. No matter what my dad did for her whether it was cooking Mexican food, showering her with gifts, or just generally trying to manage her moods, none of it was enough. All that mattered to her was a night out on the town and getting drunk. It's not a strange thing for an alcoholic to prioritize alcohol over anything and anybody else who should in the normal mind be more important but it is devastating to feel it in your own heart how little you mean to someone compare to a bottle of whiskey.

One night she left to hit the club and we didn't see her again for an entire year. She never popped in during that year nor did she call or write. My dad was crushed inside. He was desolately in despair. He didn't know what to do and on many gloomy and melancholy nights he told me and my siblings how helpless and inadequate he felt.

My brother and sisters and I were heartbroken as well. Even though not having to listen to the war of the Chapas was nice, we missed her so much. She was our mother nonetheless. While she was gone, she was missed. Because of her negligence, my brother and sisters and I had to be split up. My sisters went to Michigan and my brother stayed with my dad. I was forced to go to Texas. At one time, I had happily dreamed of going down to my grandma's house to stay for the entire summer but now when the moment finally arrived I felt sad inside because I worried that I wouldn't see my family again.

There was no way around it though; it just had to be done. I had to go see what it was like to be a cotton picker. After all, it was in my roots. Besides, my dad was in such a terrible place after she left him again that he needed time to rebuild a new life for us. My dad told us many stories about our grandpa Jesus. He used to point at me and say,

"Grandpa looked just like you, Damy. You could be twins. He was a *guero*[19] just like you. He was a very proud, illegal Mexican who picked cotton and then started his own business. Damy, you will be all right there. Go to my mother's house for summer. I will do everything I can to get us out of this mess. I promise I will come and get you when things are better."

---

[19] Mexican slang for 'white boy'.

He cried and held me in his arms. I was his little *'pollo'*, his little chicken. He pinched my cheek and the tears ran down his face. It was a picture I'll never forget nor will I ever forget the last moment before I said goodbye when I looked at his arms and caught a glimpse of a tattoo that simply said "Rico".

CHAPTER SIX

Robstown, Texas

In many respects, the scenery of Robstown, Texas, is so contrary to that of Columbus, Ohio. If you look at a map of Texas it almost seems as if Robstown hardly exists as I-69E, which parallels with US-77, crosses Route 44 making it seem as if Robstown is nothing more than an intersection in the middle of Southeast Texas. It's only a few hours north of the border from Mexico. It forms a cross. It almost seems as if there's hardly anything but those two major roads to this remote *Tejano* town but naturally there's more to Robstown than that.

No doubt, it's a cotton picker's town. In fact, they even have a stadium called Cotton Picker Stadium on Bosquez Street in northwest Robstown. Right off Bosquez Street across from Cotton Picker Stadium is Chapa Street named after my family. The fact that a street was named after us should give you the idea that our family name most definitely has roots in Robstown.

It was never a place of wealth as the houses and buildings back in my grandfather's day bore witness to. Some homes were more like shacks placed straight on the dirt than houses build on solid foundation. Its buildings are predominately short which gives a feel of being back home in a time far away from modern-day America. The Mexican District was plagued by extreme poverty, nonetheless its inhabitants knew how to celebrate life. It's the Mexican spirit that kept, and keeps, the colorful life going. The housing, that many Mexican laborers lived in back in the 1930s, 40s, and 50s, were in such poor condition that I'm not sure they would even allow that today.

Mexican Labor Housing. Robstown, TX. 1939.

The housing accommodations for the Mexicans were basically shacks made of wood with aluminum roofs built back-to-back like long rows of storage facilities. The roads were unpaved, dusty dirt roads. The doors and windows in these shacks were made of wood as well. Nobody bothered to put in glass windows. If you wanted fresh air or you just wanted to look out the window you just opened it. There was not much to look at anyway as the proximity of the next building across from you was only a few feet away. Electricity was scare too. Modern

169

commodities such as refrigerators and stoves were of very poor conditions if they even had them at all. And forget about washers and dryers in the houses. You hang out your close for the sun to dry it. The white neighborhoods were different but this was life for most Mexicans in those days.

Because of the terrible infrastructure and unpaved dirt roads, sewage and drainage caused problems for many Mexicans living in the poorest of the poorest *barrios*. *Barrio* is the Spanish word for neighborhood. Many Mexican Americans just use the Spanish word. It's associated with 'home' and being of Mexican blood. Mexicans came to work for the white man but the white man never bothered to provide basic sanitation. Robstown wasn't the only place in the United States in those days that suffered from these inhuman conditions. The history of the living conditions of the Chicanos in Southern California tells the same tale and was a major political issue for many years as Mexicans were looked down upon as the poor man who lived in horrible conditions. But let's face a fact that no one can deny; it was impossible for the Mexican immigrant to build his own infrastructure and construct his own sewage system living up to the codes of his new country. So, the white community indirectly, and some may argue deliberately, kept the Mexican immigrants down for a long time until the civil rights movements began to turn things around. Nearly half a century went by before that happened though.

But back to old Robstown; this kind of laborer housing was uninsulated. At night in the winter time, it was very cold. Only the heat in each unit that they could make kept them warm. Contrarily in the summer, it was blazing hot, nearly unbearable as the heat couldn't escape the house.

Because these units were made of wood, it was also a huge fire hazard to live there. As I said, there was no electricity in those days, no modern stove but an old-fashioned range heated by the wood you burn underneath the cooking range. If one unit caught on fire everybody on the block was in serious trouble as the flames would spread rapidly like wildfire. Back then, and especially in this type of impoverished housing, there were no such thing as fireproof, concrete walls separating one unit from the other. The modern-day building codes, which includes codes pertaining to firewalls separating one unit from the other, were unheard of in those days.

When I arrived in Robstown in the late 1970s, I was a young boy. I was twelve years old and time and living conditions for most Mexicans, whether they were legal immigrants or illegals, had changed since the early twentieth century days. I remember sitting in the Greyhound bus riding through streets lined with towering palm trees and as I sat there, I took in all the new impressions. The bus was filled with people from my dad's culture. It was my father's culture that was about to be introduced to me. I felt connected to my Mexican roots through him and his family yet this was all brand new to me. I was so mesmerized by my surroundings that it would have taken a splash of water to the face to wake me up from my daydream. I was so far removed from the hell I had lived with in my parent's home where screaming was a daily dosage like nasty medicine you just do not want to take but you cannot escape.

I can envision my first impression of Robstown, of my grandparent's homestead, as if it were just yesterday that I drove through there. It was a comforting feeling of passing cars driven by brown faces and I was thinking to myself 'This is where I belong. This is who I belong to. This is home'. This new, warm society seemed to have been waiting for me and was now opening its arms to welcome me.

I was sitting on the bus surrounded by my people and I distinctly remember the wonderful feeling of acceptance. Growing up, I always felt closer to my Chicano roots because they were the people who never failed me during challenging times. The Latino sense of solidarity and unity with their own people is so profound and so dissimilar to that of whites. Latinos are always there for each other like *hermanos*[20]. The people who showed me empathy, who showed me kindness, who taught me

---

[20] 'brothers'.

what it meant to be humble, these people were my real family, my blood. The calming face of my uncle Alex would always appear to me metaphorically when I spoke with my people.

Latinos have a unique ability to be happy even during the toughest times. They are the ultimate optimists and I always admired this trait and tried to emulate it as I became of age. I never saw the same thing with my mom's side of the family. It's amazing that families can be so totally different, nearly incomparable, just based on culture itself.

The ancient, indigenous civilizations such as the Aztecs and Mayans were some of the most advanced cultures to date and without a doubt their wisdom was passed down to future generations. From early on, Mexicans have always been a people easily adapting to life's changes. Perhaps this is one of the great traits passed down to modern day Mexicans from the Aztecs whose philosophy was focused on ethics and morality; to continuously find balance in life's changes.

My uncle Alex embodied this wisdom and he wore it on his face. There was a mysterious intensity lurking behind his eye and he had a comforting smile that made him relatable. In Ohio, the people lived simple lives, not really moving forward nor especially blessed with an ancient past to live vicariously through. Compared to Texas life, it can be a bit stagnant in Ohio like circular motions going around and round in the same routine with a sort of grey tones to life whereas in Texas the daily life of the Latinos is spiced with more colorful lifestyles in which appreciation for life in the moment is valued greater than in Ohio.

The Latino culture is warmer and more welcoming than white culture. You feel it almost immediately upon arrival. It's in the air. The Latinos are in many respects the opposite of Caucasian culture. There is something fresh, exotic, and exciting about the way they live their lives. The way of life permeates even the way that they dress wearing fashionable suits and flashy cowboy hats. They have a passion for life that you won't find in other places in North America. It's a wonderful world to be a part of and for me, arriving in Robstown, this new lifestyle was breathtaking and wondrous. I practically inhaled the spirit of the Latino culture upon arrival. It was so otherworldly compared to where I came from and I felt as if a new life for me was about to begin taking me by the storm.

Everyone here spoke Spanish. I was the only *guero* on the bus. Despite this, I felt more comfortable being here far removed from the alcohol influenced verbal and sometimes even physical abuse that my parents spewed at one another too regularly. I was alone on the Greyhound bus yet I felt that I was part of something meaningful as opposed to what I had been a part of up until this point in my life.

This was an important turning point in my young life. All these people by my side had a calm appearance that rubbed off on me. Their presence made me feel safe and at home. I admired the Latino cultures' emphasis on respect. Numerous times, had I witnessed selfless and compassionate acts by Latinos, something I find to be in stark contrast to many Caucasians I have met in my life both during my childhood and in my adult life.

I remember sitting in a Columbus bus once when a little boy was crying. None of the white people seemed to have any empathy for the little boy. As a matter of fact, they seemed quite uncomfortable and irritated as if a boy's crying was an aggravation, an annoyance of sorts, and reason for shunning and rejection. But on this bus, I was witness to something utterly different and admirable.

None of the Latinos were negatively affected in the least by the sounds of children crying. They remained calm, levelheaded, and composed as well as compassionate. The Latin culture highly values and protects the weak and innocent. It upholds dignity and respect for elders as well as comfort for those who have suffered. It's a very collectivistic society whereas the white United States is a very individualistic society. And it shows.

In Latin culture, there is an appreciation for the wisdom elders bring to the young generation. It's passed down through stories and myths. The sound of the little boy crying was quickly alleviated by a Mexican man who began to play his guitar in the back of the bus where the little boy was sitting. As he soothingly began to play his guitar, he sang an old Mexican folk song. The sound of the guitar and his voice quickly ceased the boy's crying. It had a calming effect on sad boy. I would never have witnessed something like this in Columbus. It was quite beautiful in fact how a total stranger has it in his heart to do something for someone else who has no relation to him whatever just to make the little boy feel better. Such an act of selflessness is rarely seen in most parts of the United States but in the Latino community you will find it.

The Mexican man's calming and soothing song didn't just affect the little boy. At the same time, it helped me forget about my family and the struggles I had faced up until then. Suddenly, the pain of the past began to evaporate. It was as if a knot in my chest that had been present for so long suddenly loosened up and disappeared. It had a liberating effect on me and for a moment I felt at peace with myself.

I was now entering the Latino world. It was a world my pops knew wholeheartedly and had taught us about since we were young. He spoke of the cotton pickers and how they worked tirelessly until their hands became scarred and calloused due to demanding labor conditions. On this bus, most of the Mexicans were cotton or grape pickers. The rest of the people worked at King's Grainery. I know because my Mexican family later explained it.

King's Grainery was owned by an old *gringo* businessman who gave jobs to many Mexicans who crossed the border. He had employed a very smart lady as an accountant for his business, my aunt Lilly Chapa. Lilly was all grown up now and lived a respectable life which she had earned through hard work and education. My grandmother made sure she stayed in school. Lilly worked her tail off to become a successful accountant.

My grandfather Jesus had passed away early on due to complications with diabetes. He had lived a very fulfilling life and gained a great amount of respect in his hometown. It wouldn't have surprised me in the least had a monument been erected in his memory. Unfortunately, my grandpa's life came to an end at the age of only fifty-two. My grandma Juanita was loved dearly by all her children throughout her life. The unexpected and early passing of my grandpa was hard for Juanita not only emotionally but also financially as grandpa had always, as was customary in those days and particularly in Latino societies, been the provider of the family.

I remember my dad wired her money from time to time when he had the means to do so. It is customary and expected in the Hispanic cultures that the younger generation pitch in and help take care of their parents in their old age or during any challenging times in life. It's a sign of love and respect that most western cultures today lack grossly.

We've become selfish and too focused on meeting and exceeding our own personal goals in life. This is not just the case in the United States but also in Europe. Meanwhile, we tend to forget where we came from and the gift of life that our parents have given us. I am in much favor of the Latin way of caretaking of our parents, even though admittedly my relationship with my mother was next to non-existing. I cannot help that she rejected us thinking more of her own needs that those of her children. You cannot hold on to someone who doesn't want to stay. You can only love them while it lasts.

In any event, my grandpa Jesus was no longer there to support my grandma. He was not able to provide for her anymore as his candle had burned out long before it should. My grandma was left in a tough situation. She was never the 'go-getter' type. Her new life without her love, Jesus, was very intimidating to her as she now had to figure out a way to support herself. As is tradition in most Mexican families, her job had always been to take care of her family whereas Jesus' job was to bring in the money to support the family.

There is a clear division of labor and responsibilities in Mexican families. In many respects, I think it's admirable that the Mexican culture aims to uphold the traditional values of family as opposed to modern, western societies where women try to dominate. Sometimes the modern lifestyle leaves the man to feeling inadequate and it can make him want to leave to seek ways in which he can feel adequate.

The clear division of male and female roles helps uphold the values of a traditional family structure where the father is the gatherer and the mother is the nurturer. But with Jesus gone, my grandma now had more weight on her shoulders than she was prepared for financially. She felt pressured to take on everything suddenly on her own and she needed the help of her children.

This was nothing new for many Mexican-American families, however. They had grown accustomed to these sorts of challenges and adapted to change well but that does not mean that the changes they were forced to deal with were easy nor without pain in one's heart. As I said, in the Latino culture it was, and relatively so still is, common for the young generation to be taken care of by their elders often until marriage, and likewise it's common for the young to then take care of their elders in old age. It is a natural cycle of life that was established back in ancient times.

I've come to realize that Mexican people have the most respect for people out of any culture that I know of. Controversial issues such as that of abortion are particularly frowned upon amongst Latinos even in the roughest Mexican-American neighborhoods. We celebrate life to the fullest so it is considered a profound lack of respect for human life to abort a child.

Children are a gift and their precious life should always be cherished and welcomed. I'm like that with my own children as well and not just because I aim to be a much better parent than my mom ever was but also because I believe life is truly a gift from God. No matter the amount of suffering required, whether it was working fifteen hour days in the blazing hot sun picking cotton for the white man or cleaning the white lady's house, Mexicans are always ready to face new challenges and do everything that stands in their power to ensure the protection of their family, including if exposed to violence.

These lovely people are a part of my lineage, my destiny, and my culture. Even though I physically looked more like my mother with the light hair, blue eyes, and fair complexion I had nothing in common with her side of the family. We were so estranged it's not even funny. Something inside me longed to be accepted by my Mexican brethren. They were the ones who showed me warmth when my pale skinned mother showed me coldness. Being Chicano is not just a matter of skin color. It is who you are on the inside that matters. In our culture, we refer to it as 'Being brown on the inside'. It's a mentality, a way of life that most other cultures don't quite understand to its fullest.

In my debut movie *Blood In Blood Out,* there is a line that perfectly fits how I feel: "White on the outside and brown on the inside".

When I was awoken on the bus, the only other person left was the Mexican guitarist. He was strumming a soothing rhythm until my attention shifted to the sound of my aunt Lilly outside the bus shouting, "Damy! Damy! Come outside of the bus!" She was waving at me welcoming me to what would be my home, my Mexican home, for the next few months. It was going to become the best months in all my childhood. I was looking forward to spending time with my Mexican family even though it had broken my heart to say 'goodbye' to my dad in Ohio knowing his pain after mother once again had abandoned us and screwed dad over taking all his hard-earned money that he had saved up. Nonetheless, a new, exciting chapter of my life was about to begin.

My aunt was waiting at the bus station with my grandmother. They wore colorful, floral dresses. They were Mexican-American dresses that they bought from a small *tienda* located on a tiny street full of discount merchants. This store was a microcosm of a 1970's version of the store *Ross Dress For Less.* Typically, the dresses were accessorized with large Mexican jewelry.

As soon as I arrived there, my aunt Lilly and grandmother had an astonished look on their faces when they saw the condition of my clothing. I looked indistinguishably like a kid who had just escaped an orphanage. I was practically a male version of Annie, the little red-haired orphan from the musical. The only difference was that I was a boy and not ginger.

All my possessions fit into a brown paper bag. There were only three t-shirts and one pair of jeans that were a size too small. My mother's negligence of taking proper care of my needs was at fault for the way I was dressed. She was hardly ever around and would rather spend her money on alcohol than clothes for her children. My dad was too busy making a living to support us so certain things, such as shopping for children's clothes, he didn't do nor did he notice the condition they were in.

I put the blame on my mom completely. She lived her life solely for her own enjoyment. She exhibited very little empathy for anyone, almost to the point of sociopathic behavior. While I hold her accountable for the neglect, at the same time I feel sorry for her. It's a dilemma that on the one hand I'm very upset with her and on the other hand I understand how she became as messed up as she was. It always comes back to this again and again.

I know it should repetitive but she really was a sad product of her environment suffering abuse by her parents and uncles. You can say that she was predispositioned to failure as a parent because in all fairness she was never taught the correct way to be a mother by anyone. She had no good, or even somewhat decent, role model to mirror herself in. Her mother didn't take her clothing shopping and her father much less. It was a vicious family cycle that we had been locked into and were forced to pay the price of. My dad did his best to keep us together as a family but Donna Mañana was never satisfied and there was nothing he could do to cast out the demons from Donna's past.

You cannot change the past. The past remains the past. It's history. You can only work toward a better future by making conscious decisions in the present. My dad tried so hard to make decisions that would improve our position in life but his hard work so often failed because Donna and Rico never shared the same vision. My dad was much more long-sighted than she ever was. She lived in the moment of 'free, white, and twenty-one' and she continuously failed to give us a proper childhood. It's unfathomable the amount of times us kids were left with dirty clothes, cockroach infested rooms, or broken bottles lying on the floor which we had to carefully tip-toe around to not cut ourselves. God forbid if we did cut ourselves on her broken bottles because Lord knows she was never around to help us much less take us to the hospital if needed. She was simply incapable of living up to the responsibilities of being a parent. She had no idea how to properly raise children. She never learned nor did she care to learn to be a parent. And upon my arrival in Robstown it really became clear to me.

My Grandma and aunt Lilly talked to each other in Spanish for a moment. I remember them speaking about my mother. Though I wasn't fluent, I was able to understand a great deal of what they said due to the time I had spent listening to my dad's fluent Spanish. My grandmother was held in the highest regard by everyone in the family. Unrivaled self-respect was characteristic of her persona. She always thought of others before herself.

Flashing back, I remember one time when from a distance, I saw my grandma picking out clothes for me. I turned to walk back into the living room. They're just glimpses like still pictures of past moments that hang on. They're not necessarily cohesive but remember that it was so long ago that this happened. In fact, we're talking about forty years or so. Later that evening, I remember the smell of my grandma's Mexican food. I could smell the corn in the tortillas which can only be described as an unforgettable experience. I can still hear mariachis playing in the background. This was my dad's birth place. This was the town of the cotton pickers. The one and only Robstown, Texas.

CHAPTER SEVEN

Discovering My Chicano Roots

Every morning, a radio station playing the tunes of my grandmother's favorite Mexican songs woke me up. The popular hits sounding on the radio entertained me. It was so otherworldly compared to what I had known so far in my life in the Northeast of the United States. Down in Texas, and particularly this part of Texas, it was a different atmosphere all together.

Freddy Fender was my favorite Mexican musician of that era. He was a true Tejano hero from San Benito, Texas who represented a lot of what the cotton picker stood for. He represented not only the American Dream for many but also the Mexican American Dream because of the way he had worked his way out of poverty. He was an inspiration to millions of Mexican followers.

One of his most well-known hits was *Before the Next Teardrop Falls.* This song seemed to always come on when I wasn't thinking about my painful childhood. It was a very heartfelt song with that Texas felt tune to it that characterizes country western songs of that era particularly. Although it was a beautiful and paradoxically sad love song that he sang in both English and Spanish making it so much more *de su corazón*,[21] unfortunately it also always reminded me of my parents' constant battles. The words of *Before the Next Teardrop Falls* used to echo in my head going like this:

If he brings you happiness
Then I wish you both the best
If it's happiness that matters most of all
But if he ever breaks your heart
If a teardrop ever start
I'll be there before the next teardrop falls

That song made me think of the sleepless nights when I huddled closely to my brother and sisters as we were forced to listen to the sound of our parents physically beating the life out of each other. They seemed to have a contest as to who would cry more, who would reach their boiling point fastest.

---

[21] 'from his heart'.

There is another song of his just as popular called *Wasted Days and Wasted Nights* which resembles the chaotic relationship of my parents not to mention my dad's blues over my mom. Freddie's words rang out like this:

Wasted days and wasted nights
I have left for you behind
For you don't belong to me
Your heart belongs to someone else

Why should I keep loving you?
When I know that you're not true
And why should I call your name
When you're to blame for making me blue?

At times, their fighting exceeded the limits of what we could handle seeing and hearing. Because of their fighting, the sheriffs' office was called on a regular basis. When shit really hit the fan in my house, the cops would eventually bust in the door and yell out loud while us kids were trying, though unavoidably, to shield ourselves from the commotion,

"Put your hands up, Sir!" they yelled at my dad as if he was the only culprit in the house and my mom was the pure victim.

"This is my house, you understand that! You can't just come in here like that," my dad screamed back at the police in defense,

The police, who had been there before trying to separate my parents and prevent them from halfway killing each other, replied as standard answer to a domestic dispute call,

"Sir, the people next door called us. They said they heard a woman screaming loud!"

It's typical that the cops almost automatically and without even first assessing the situation objectively take the women in defense as if women cannot resort to violent behavior. When they hear women screaming, everybody resolutely thinks the man is beating the shit out of a defenseless, poor woman. It pretty much never occurs to anyone that women in fact can be, if not just as violent then at least, aggressive and vicious just the same.

"That's because my wife has a big mouth!" my dad yelled back at the police officers.

All too often, my mom would be holding a glass of Seagram's 7 as her demeanor suddenly changed upon the police officers' arrival.

"Would you officers just let us be?" she calmly told the officers while waiving her glass around typically already drunk off her ass. She didn't try to act the victim. She just wanted them to know that they were in control of the fight and just wanted to be left alone to battle out their differences.

My parents were so selfish that all they cared about now was for the cops to leave so they could get back to their alcoholic induced party while infuriating each other more and more. My siblings and I were hiding behind the corridor that lead to the kitchen and we thanked God that the cops had arrived to calm the madness just a little bit. It was torture to have to listen to our parents battling each other with harsh words and hatred accusing each other of everything under the sun.

In the heat of the fights they, forgot all about us kids. They had no consideration in that moment of how this madness affected us nor how it scared us for life. You can try to hide your pain. You can try to forget what happened, repress it, even deny it but the fact of the matter is that the ghost of the past is with you no matter what you do. It's right under the surface and rears its ugly face from time to time bringing back memories of the past, of your early years. Sometimes it even permeates involuntarily your own behavior in moments that resembles those you've seen so many years ago, you want to let go of the past, of the memories, but it's not that easy. It's not that simple.

Through these nights at the madhouse that we grew up in, all we wanted was to have a normal life but it wasn't meant to be. All we wanted was a mom and dad to come home to who would help us with our school work, play with us, and prepare us for life ahead in a normal, calm, and constructive way. But our parents were like oil and water or light and darkness. They did not complement each other in the least.

At this point in my life, my ulcer problem had become a serious health risk. I treated myself with milk and magnesium but it only took away the pain on occasion. Fortunately, moving to Robstown even though it only was for a few months allowed me to escape by problems and permitted a steady healing of my ulcer.

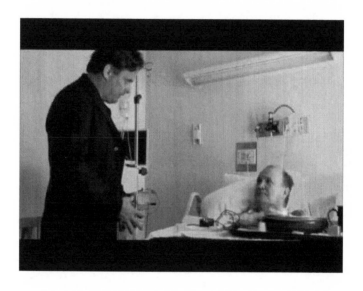

With my dad in the hospital toward the end of his life.

Me at 15 years old. My .357 was hidden in my jacket. My uncle Bobby is on the right.

My grandma Juanita Chapa.

My grandpa Jesus Chapa. The real thing.

Married to Natasha Henstridge right after Blood In Blood Out.

Me, Karina Lombard (star of Legends of the Fall) and my cousin Mark Chapa (son of a hitman).

My father being arraigned. This is the real thing.
Not a movie.

My real life gangster father, Rico Chapa.

Rico Chapa's mugshot smiling like Al Capone when the FBI arrested him on bookmaking charges.

Ronaldo "Rico" Chapa upon his release from jail.

Uncle Jesse, Aunt Norma, Grandma Juanita, Uncle Bobby, Uncle Johnny and Rico Chapa.

Uncle Kiki. Known for organized crime and being a hitman.

Me on the film set of "El Chicano" in Hollywood in 2010.

In Robstown, it was only the blues sung by Freddie Fender that brought back memories. My mom, as I said, had taken off with my dad's savings. Two thousand dollars was gone. That was messed up but it wasn't the first time she had done that. For me, however, Robstown was a long-needed break from hell and drunkenness.

My aunt Lilly continued to work at King's Granery. Her boss, Mr. King, greatly appreciated her and she had by now become his favorite employee, and for good reason. My grandmother used to tell me that Lilly was a natural multi-tasker and efficiently handled mountains of paperwork in record time.

My grandma and my aunt Lilly always tried to bring the best out of me and to push me to do better.

"Damy, Damy! Get up, *Mijo, Levántese! Tu abuela tiene migas, mijito. Y hay pan de dulce,"*[22] my grandma said as she woke me up announcing that breakfast was ready Mexican style.

"*Qué abuela?*[23]" I asked drowsily.

One of my favorite Mexican dishes was *Migas.* It's an egg and tortilla mix that sometimes include hot dogs. It was a spectacular breakfast and a

---

[22] 'Mijo (meaning my son in an endearing way), get up! Your grandma has migas, my little boy. And there's sweet bread her.'
[23] 'What, grandma?'

delicious hot meal at any time. Sometimes I used to think that there was an almost healing effect to grandma's *migas*, although logically and scientifically that isn't the case naturally, but as you recall I suffered terribly from ulcers as a young child.

The ulcer had a painful and brutal side effect from the constant stress caused by my dysfunctional home life. It caused me to throw up blood on many occasions. Though there's medical treatment to be obtained to treat ulcers, I didn't have the luxury of receiving medical attention at the time. It might not even have alleviated the condition anyway because of the ongoing fights between my parents.

Nevertheless, something happened shortly after I arrived at my grandma's house in Texas, far away from the chaos in Ohio. My grandma's tender, loving care and her amazing homemade Mexican cooking made the vomiting of blood stop after only a week's time. I savored her *migas* and even much more so after my ulcer healed.

My grandmother's house was such a liberating experience. It was a complete contrast to that of my mother's which was filled with water bugs and roaches, mice and sometimes even rats.

My mom was not exactly the most Christian woman in the world. In fact, she despised Christian beliefs. My dad took great offense to her aversion to the Christian beliefs because he was raised with fundamental Christian beliefs himself, a Catholic by heart, and wanted to pass on to his children what were very valuable lessons in life to him.

They argued about religion constantly. My mom changed religion from time to time. There were some strange symbols from different religions. At one point, she became obsessed with the hexagram and to put a giant one in our window. As commonly known, the hexagram is a sign of witchcraft which was brought to famous status by Alister Crowley. My dad objected to it and they could never seem to find a happy medium respecting each other's different points of views. In his mind, growing up Catholic, artifacts of the Lord on the walls were important to him as they gave him the peace of mind knowing that God and Jesus were with him and that is what he wanted his children to grow up knowing and believing. For my mom, she despised the thought of Jesus. She did everything she could to keep us from it. She was very vehement regarding Christ. This separated her and I even more than we were already. Later, we became estranged. My mother was very confused. I remember late in life as she was dying, I tried to visit her. I had just gotten out of prison for false accusations by one of my ex-girlfriends. My ex-girlfriend was trying to control our child and my visitation with him. This happens all the time. In any event, I had been in prison in Germany and had just been out for two months. That story is a whole other book. I went home to my sister's house. She helped me but I went to my mother's house to try to patch thing up from years of separation.

It was surreal to me. I looked at her. I was in her home and we were trying as hard as we could in front of my other family members to be kind to each other. But there had always been animosity between us so thick that you could cut it with a knife.

I was looking through some old documents and pictures in a box. I looked down and saw a picture of my Granny, her grandmother. I also saw a confirmation into the Pentecostal faith. I looked toward my mother and asked her if Granny was really a Christian and that that was great.

My mother gave me the chills. She looked over at me now aged. Her piercing blue eyes and tilted head was positioned as if in a horror film.

"No, she was not," she replied.

"Here is her confirmation into the Church" I said.

My sister walked in and interrupted us.

"You two, stop now while you can."

"Okay, okay," I said. I had just had a traumatic event. I needed all the friends I could get at this point. At the time, I had some minor business problems and I was suffering from PTSD from being thrown in jail on false accusations. Later, the Bavarian State paid me thousands of Euros in pain and suffering retribution for wrongful imprisonment on false accusations. However, it was definitely not enough for what they did to me. In answering my mom's rejection, it was hell for a while but for once I didn't stand up to fight for the truth nor to fight her as I usually would have done. I just looked at my mother and said, "As you wish."

I put my Granny's confirmation certificate away and I looked up and saw that my son was watching TV. I looked behind him and there was my mother staring at me. It was the strangest thing. She was staring deep into my eyes. Her left hand was erect and she made the Satanic devil horns sign toward me.

"What the hell are you doing?" I looked at her inquiringly. My son looked at my mother and she swiftly dropped her hand.

"Why did you do that?" I wanted to know.

"What? What?" my son asked.

I didn't want to bring him into the drama. I looked at my mother and said to him that it was nothing and that everything was fine. I told him she needed her IV changed.

At this point in time, she was literally dying. That night, I looked in the place where she kept her books. One of them was about demons. Underneath the word 'demon' was a picture of me on some movie set somewhere. I was looking at it when she entered the room. I felt desperate. I needed a place to stay. I was not about to bring up her eccentric ways. I was more desperate now after what had happened to me in Munich, Germany and needed anyone with a kind heart. I needed a friend, family, anyone.

I looked at her as hard as it was. After nearly forty years living on my own, I did not want to ask my mother for anything. But I was desperate. My children were with me and I was alone with them. I had to do it.

"Mom, can I stay in one of your extra bedrooms?"

I don't know why but my old, favorite movie *Amadeus* came to mind. It flashed before my eyes.

The part where Amadeus played by Tom Hulce asks his rival Salieri for a loan. In the movie, he went from 200 duckets to 100 duckets to 50 duckets, all to no avail. I looked intensely into my mother's blue eyes.

"Answer me. I need a place" I demanded. She looked at me with a coldness I can only describe coming from a dark cave.

"No, you cannot. My husband..." she began. I looked at her again and then down the hallway with the empty rooms. I walked out and never saw her again after that. My dear sister, Cita, took it upon herself and her good Christian heart to take my children and myself into her home for a while until I got better. I never forgot that chilling look my mother gave me. Still, I forgive her. she taught me that, the cold stare. She must have.

My grandma Juanita was a true Christian woman. She devoutly walked to church daily come rain or shine. Her house was decorated with pictures of Jesus and alongside those framed pictures were photos of her husband Jesus. I had always been told that I looked very like my grandfather Jesus which was something that made me feel proud.

Grandma Juanita

Completely contrary to my mother, my Grandmother had prominent Indian features. She had dark, wise, deep-set eyes that only Indians have and she had those very high cheek bones characteristic of Aztec and Mayan features. She had an omnipotent aura about her as if she could see right through you. Nevertheless, she was a very humble woman and always very serious like my uncle Alex, whom I loved dearly too. They were to me what represented ancient Aztec descent. There was something genuine about her. It was in her face, in her eyes. I'll never forget staring into her deep, piercing black eyes and feeling a sense of warmth radiate from their aura. I remember feeling like I finally had a real mother.

Her appearance gave me comfort. I felt her compassion, motherliness, empathy, and love. I never got that from my mom. For once in my life, I could relate to what normal kids feel being raised in a normal home. I felt I belong. I felt welcomed, wanted, and loved.

I longed for a real mother. My mom always had an aversion toward me and my younger brother. I don't recall her ever hugging me, something all children need from their parents. Do you know what it's like never to be hugged by your mother? It was different with Ricco. I never understood why and I still don't but my mother loved Ricco without a doubt. I don't think she ever truly loved me.

It made no sense to me. In my mind, we were all siblings and deserved the same love but you don't choose to be loved by a parent. You cannot make someone love you if they just don't. Maybe it was his looks. Whatever the reason was, she obviously preferred one child over the others. I suffered from her lack of love for me.

She had an affinity for anything Italian. Maybe Ricco appeared more Italian than the rest of us. If that's the case, I think I might have connected the dots between her love for him and not us. His Italian looks might have appealed to her as it was something that she always loved while the rest of us were Mexican in her eyes and somehow beneath her ideal human being. It was the same issue she had with my dad. She felt he tricked her. As if he had swindled her into believing that he was Italian only for her to later learn he was Mexican. She always hated him for that.

It's painful to realize your mother basically categorized her kids in something like a cast system but she did always hate my dad for making her believe he was Italian. But we suffered from it too, her discontentment with him. It was like a domino effect. And so, her discontentment with the fact that most of us kids weren't of the ideal human race permeated her attitude towards us.

Some have said she suffered from multiple personality disorder caused by the abused she endured in her early years. She had a very dark past that I don't think any one of us were ever able to really get to the bottom of. However, she seemed obsessed with certain dates and seemed to try to get all our birthdays as close to Halloween as possible, although it was only the boys that were born within a couple of day from October 31st. One of my little sisters was born on October 18th but the interesting thing is that she was two weeks premature. Thus, the boys' birthdays are all within a day of each other; two of us on October 29th and the last brother on October 30th.

It's a big mystery in our family. Some say it was related to *Illuminati* and certain rituals performed around those dates but in the end my mother never fully let us in on her gloomy and gruesome past. Today, these bleak and grim secrets rests with her soul.

But with my grandma Juanita it was different. It was a blessing to be near her. The sun was shining and I felt a comforting beam of warmth shoot down my spine. To have a woman who loves you unconditionally was the best feeling I could have asked for. Nothing compares to that. To some people, it might sound insignificant and silly to long for a mother figure in your life, for unconditional love and care, but if you've never felt a mother's love, it is not at all insignificant, much less silly.

Unless you've been there, you really cannot understand what it means to miss having a mother who will tug you in at night as she kisses you good night telling you she loves you and how special you are to her. The sweet, little kisses that a mother places gently on her child's head mean so much more than words can ever express. My grandma was so utterly different in every way from my mother. She fascinated me, not just in term of the love she had for me but also as I watched her carefully prepare my food. It was a genuine love like no other love I had ever felt before.

CHAPTER EIGHT

The Smell of Sweet Bread

My grandmother made it her goal to teach me Spanish. It was a good thing and not only because I've used it since then but also because she spoke very little English. Once you're put right in the situation and the person you're speaking with hardly speaks English, you're forced to learn. I was a fast learner so my Spanish skills rapidly picked up.

After what had become our ritual morning breakfast, I rushed to get dressed in my new underwear and socks. It's amazing that you can get excited about new socks and underwear but you must understand that when it's been ages since you have had new clothes these trivial things excite you. I put on a TexMex design shirt and I proudly displayed my new connection with the community. My Grandma had given me something to be proud of. On top of that, she even bought me a *ranchero* hat just like the one my grandpa had trademarked.

"*Me pareces como tu abuelo, mijo,*" she used to tell me in Spanish meaning 'you look like your grandpa'. Every time she compared me to my grandpa I felt an intense sense of belonging, a real sense of pride that I had not felt before in my life. There was a connection that I had not felt before up north. Gradually, my self-confidence grew every day as my grandma's kind words my perspective of myself and my view on life. She made me cry once when I listened to her description of how compassionately my grandpa lived his life. His life was such an inspiration. All I wanted was to be just like him when I grew up.

At this point, I had developed an intermediate understanding of Spanish. I was now able to hold a decent conversation and express more detailed what I wanted to say. I had gained the confidence to initiate conversation and not just listen and do the 'aha' thing that you often do when you're just starting out learning a language. One day, I began to talk to her about my home life back in Ohio.

"*Mi madre y mi padre tienen muchos problemas, abuela,[24]*" I said to her letting her in on my secret about my concerns with my parents. I'm sure she knew already from my dad that things weren't exactly rosy and idyllic but I hadn't talked to her about my feelings before. I didn't want to hang out my laundry but I also needed to get the load off my shoulders. It was weighing heavily on me and, as I said, had caused me to have an ulcer.

"*Oigame, mijo. Escuchame una cosa. Ahorita estás con tu abuela. No estás con esos problemas. ¿Que descansas, me entiendes?[25]*" she calmingly said and gently comforted me that things were better now here at grandma's house and I need not worry.

It felt good to know that my problems weren't in my face anymore and that I could relax and enjoy life in a way I couldn't do back in Ohio.

---

[24] "My mother and father have many problems, grandma".
[25] "Listen, my dear. Hear me out. Right now, you're with your grandma. You're not with your problems. You need to relax, you understand me?"

"*Mijito*, come to me. I know what will make you feel better; *pan dulce*," she interjected and she was right because there's nothing that can make you forget your problems like the sweet and delicious taste of *pan dulce* with that amazing hint of cinnamon. Right out of the oven, they are downright incredible and grandma's *pan dulce* was like nothing I'd ever had before in my own house. My Mother was never one to make homemade bread or pastries. She didn't care to cook just the basic, homemade meals so grandma's kitchen was pure luxury and I enjoyed every minute of it.

My grandma was always very protective of me and concerned with my well-being. I guess for good reasons too. She used to hold my hand tightly as we crossed busy streets. She always kept a caring eye on me to make sure I was okay. This is what a mother should do but something I wasn't used to; however, it was very nice and comforting to know that I was in good hands when I was with my grandma. The harsh life at home having to take care of myself and my siblings when dad was working and mom was either passed out in her bedroom or not there at all made me grow up faster than any kid should but at grandma's house things were different. I could be a kid again knowing that there was an adult looking out for me. I'm not even sure how she was ever able to sleep! To me it seemed that she must have been sleeping with one eye always open.

Everybody around us spoke Spanish. Wherever we went, the people we would pass on our way spoke next to no English. Of course, that was a good thing for me because every day my Spanish improved. I guess I stood out a little compared to other kids with my light features and blue eyes in a world where nearly everybody had black hair and brown eyes.

There was one lady that could not resist the temptation. She just had to pinch my rosy-red cheeks. My grandmother was so proud of me. She used to display me like a badge of honor. For once, it was so nice to feel wanted and appreciated by a woman. All the attention she brought upon me as a child, determined the path I took later in life which was that of a thespian, always seeking attention and trying to realize my dreams through acting and drama. In a sense, she was the foundation of my future.

Robstown was a small city characterized by familial ties. It was a place where it seemed as if everyone knew each other. It was a tight-knit community and this was possible due to its size. In larger cities, this closeness of a community isn't possible quite the same way. Robstown was completely otherworldly in comparison to cow-town Columbus, Ohio that I grew up in as a child. To most however, Columbus at the time was still considered the New York City of the Midwest. Robstown had a more peaceful presence and a vibrancy that you could sense in the air on hot summer nights than most other places. I knew I was never going to feel this comfortable, nor this happy ever again. It left a unique impression on me that I have taken with me throughout my life. I savored these precious moments hoping they would last forever. Up until that point, my childhood had offered me nothing but misery, pain, and frustration. There was only a handful of times that I remember feeling good living with my parents.

My grandmother became my saving grace. She opened a whole new world of opportunities that I carried with me in my life. Her actions were a constant inspiration to me and her compassion combined with the inspiring atmosphere of Robstown set me on an endless path to express myself through creativity. She became the role model I never had. In her presence, the blue sky and the green grass vividly came alive. I felt as if the sky and the grass wasn't just there. It was living and breathing just like me. Her tender loving care permeated everything such as in how she turned everyday cooking into an art made the taste of *pan dulce* and chocolate become mouth-watering memorable. Because of her, I had become fully aware of the present moment and locked into what artists and intellectuals call a "flow state".

Grandma held my hand through the darkness of my life. She was my light at the end of the tunnel and her genuine kindness helped heal my ulcer and wash away my tears. I'll never forget the poor, Mexican musicians who used to strum their guitars until their fingers bled nor will I ever forget the passionate *Latina* dancers with their colorful dresses and graceful movements that I experienced during my time staying at grandma's house. This wasn't just your average American city; this was Robstown.

The humble Mexicans in Robstown accepted me unconditionally. It didn't matter that I couldn't speak Spanish fluently yet nor that I didn't blend in amongst all their beautiful, brown faces due to my light features. They could relate to me on a non-superficial level which up until this point in my life had been foreign to me. They understood that being Chicano is not a color; it's the way you think and the way you feel. The sweet smell of *pan dulce* had changed my life forever. For the first time in my life I truly felt Chicano.

CHAPTER NINE

Being Macho

It was pitch black outside one evening when my aunt Lilly asked me if I would walk up the street to grab her an aspirin for her splitting headache. I respectfully complied. My grandma was sound asleep and probably had no idea that I went outside at night time. I'm not sure she would have approved with that had she known.

I had become used to Robstown and felt comfortable there. I loved that my grandma wanted to protect me but at the same time I relished any chance I could get to freely to go out alone whenever I wanted to. It's that natural transition from child to adolescent that sets in when you reach your early teen years. Your need to feel independent, yet protected, is part of the transformation that takes place in a young man's like, and I suppose also the lives of young girls.

My grandmother was always so protective of me to the point where I sometimes felt overly sheltered even though I know she meant well. I wasn't used to that though so sometimes it became too much but at the same time, I loved it. However, it was also time for me to gradually start becoming more independent. I was twelve and entering my teenage years so doing aunt Lilly a favor getting her the aspirins she needed for her headache was a way for me to feel independent. I was starting to pull away.

There were times when it felt strange walking out by myself in Robstown because it was completely dominated by Latinos and very contrary to Columbus, Ohio in practically every respect imaginable. I stood out with my blue eyes and blond highlights. I knew I was different but my grandma made me feel accepted. Although for the time, I had escaped the harshness of my parents' home, I still suffered from nightmares from time to time. On those cold nights, my grandma used to sleep near me to reassure me that I was safe. I needed that. Nothing was more comforting than the warmth radiating from her wrinkled, Indian face. I felt as if a person for once was interested in my well-being only and not just themselves. The unselfishness of my grandma was such a blessing to me. I was finally able to experience what a normal childhood is like. My grandmother was an expert at making me feel nurtured.

I distinctly remember the comforting atmosphere that my aunt and grandmother tried to create for me. There were crosses and burning candles, which illuminated the faces of Maria and the Saints. I felt I was in a spiritually protected place in which devils could not enter. The fight over religion had disappeared and her house was calmer and more loving. Although I loved the protectiveness of my grandma, her lovely cooking and nurturing, nonetheless, I felt a bit overprotected sometimes. I felt the need to pull away and be on my own. I needed some alone time too.

Aunt Lilly wasn't as overprotective of me. Looking back, I'm not sure what my grandmother would have said had she known aunt Lilly had allowed me to walk by myself alone in the streets of

Robstown, Texas at night. I had heard that there were parts of Robstown that were unsafe for anybody to be walking in, let alone a young kid who stood out because of his fair features but that didn't stop me from getting my aunt's aspirin. I'm a bit of a thrill seeker by nature. I like my independence so of course I relished the chance to go out and explore Robstown whenever the opportunity arose.

My aunt Lilly used to grab my hand and say, "*Mijo, ven aquí.* I want to give you something." She was always a generous person. She was ready to lend you a hand if you needed anything.

My cousin Teresa Chapa was a generous person as well. She was Chicana and her Spanish was much better than mine which was something that I admired about her besides the fact that she was very pretty. I always kept it a secret. I was too shy to talk about it when I was younger but the fact is that upon meeting her for the first time, not knowing at the time that she was my cousin, I fell deeply in love with her. I was so young and innocent then, only twelve years old. She was probably seventeen at the time. She had the most beautiful dark Latin skin. I dreamed of caressing her but I very quickly woke up from my dream when I realized that she was my cousin. This was a huge issue and I didn't want to die a premature death at the hands of one of my uncles so I quickly dropped the idea of her.

Regardless, she was imprinted in my mind as the image of how the perfect woman for me would act and look. She knew how to be strong yet remain feminine. It was a tantalizing combination that drove me crazy inside. Even when she became upset or filled with fiery passion, she was in such control of herself that she could express empathy.

I was so enthralled with her that later in life I became obsessed with finding a woman who could emulate her unique personality. She even had a slightly distinguished overbite which I was highly attracted to. She used to cook me the most mouth-watering Mexican food while she flirted with me in Spanish. Spanish is such a romantic language so the flirting in Spanish made it all the better. Of course,

237

it was all a fantasy. It was an innocent crush which I could never act upon. Almost every woman I ever loved from that point on had an overbite. It was a strange obsession that would remain with me for the rest of my life.

My aunt Lilly had a special place in my heart. She was so generous. She used to look for blue T-shirts and brown cowboy hats for me to try on so I could look like my grandpa who was my hero. Once she found a white colored TexMex cowboy hat for me. I was so proud when she placed it on my head. I thought I looked great like my grandpa. Later that day, she walked me out and asked me to grab her an aspirin from the town store. After I got to the store I remember I noticed the wondrous smell of *pan dulce* and *tamales*. That scent always stuck with me. I loved tamales so much. Nothing excited me more than the scent of fresh *tamales* made in Texas.

Los Angeles is a close runner-up to Robstown as the city with the best hot *tamales*, however, nothing compares to the spicy yet sweet Texas-made *tamales* which made my tummy jump with joy. It was like the effect that the charismatic Mexican illegals and Tex-Mex people had on my spirit. They made me feel a part of the world, a part of life, a part of something I had never been a part of before. They filled a void in my life, you may say.

My true culture began to surround me like a warm Mexican blanket on a cold desert night. It was as if I was on fire, but a pure fire, a fire of passion intertwined with love. From that grew a profound understanding of who I was and who I was supposed to become. I had found my identity; I felt Chicano.

The feeling of the Chicano spirit was overwhelming to me. It embraced me with its warmth and it taught me its family values. It showed me a different path, one that I was not aware of as the poor, light-skinned boy who was raised far from Robstown by an alcoholic mother. The feeling you have when you suddenly find the place where you belong and realize what you've been searching for, is an amazing feeling. It's like coming home after a long journey.

In that sense, Robstown was a rewarding place to come to and most people lived their lives here the right way. Of course, you had your areas, as you do in any city, where people took life for granted by turning to a life of alcoholism or deadly drug obsessions but this destructive kind of lifestyle only represented a small slice of what the Chicano culture was like during this era. For the most part, what I witnessed was love, warmth, and the ancient spirit of acceptance towards someone who was different.

There was no doubt that I was different. I had blue eyes and light skin. Interestingly, when the sun hit my skin a slight but noticeable tanned, olive hue began to appear. My mixed Mexican and Italian genes began to come out. I looked like a carbon copy of my grandfather. No longer was I just your average joe-"white boy". I had enough genes to proudly show my Latino background. That warm, beautiful skin color of Latinos came out in me as well only underlining the fact that I was more Chicano than white.

As the hot, Texas sun began to beat down on my young body I walked with my head held high down the street. I felt like a true TexMex boy for a shining moment. I had embodied a proud and strong *Tejano* sense of myself and I had finally become *the real Damian Chapa*.

I was Juanita Chapa's grandson. My self-esteem started to reveal itself. I felt strong, complete, and ready for life to bring on all its adventures. I had removed myself from the darkness of my alcoholic parents that previously had permeated my youth. Here I was in my young body ready to take on the world, happy as could be when suddenly, to my great dismay, I was pulled back into reality abruptly by the sound of a loud, screaming voice. I looked up towards the hot sun and at that time I saw a Mexican boy wearing a blue bandana.

"Esquinarme, vato?[26]*"* I looked at the boy and responded as calmly as I could because I had no idea at that moment what the guy was saying.

"Hey man, *no comprendo mucho español*," I said apologetically.

This kid appeared to be about the age of 16 years old or so. He was slender and strong with a piercing look in his eye.

"What the hell man! What the fuck is a white kid doing here?"

I looked off into the distance and saw a group of four Mexican teens who were bigger and stronger than him with their hands gripped firmly on their weapons as they stopped for a moment to catch their breath. They had been chasing after the Mexican kid in front of me. I saw some Chicano boys little ways from where I was. The tall Chicano boy started to yell.

"Hey David! Your ass is mine, *pendejo*! Who's the fucking white boy? I'll kick his ass too!"

My heart began to race. I knew I had suddenly found myself in the middle of something deep. I had no business being involved in this mess. David, the Mexican kid with the blue bandana, looked at me

---

[26] "You got my back?"

with serious eyes and if he was adamant about getting an answer from me.

"*Esquiname, vato?*"

I looked at him confused. I didn't understand what he was saying and things were suddenly happening too fast. I found myself on shaky grounds. I was entering a territory I didn't belong to at all.

"What the hell does that mean?" I yelled back.

David looked at me dead on.

"You got my back, *buey?*" he wanted to know as he translated *'esquiname'* for me. *'Vato'* is a common expression.

Buey was a word with multiple meanings I learned. The literal meaning of the word translates to goat in English but can also mean 'stud' when addressing a male. Chicanos use *buey* when they are mad, happy or just as a term of endearment. I had heard the word many times growing up so I quickly understood what he was saying. Then I looked at him with that Chapa pride that we Chapas have coming from my grandfather's courage.

"I ain't no goat, but I got your back," I said jumping into situation immediately.

I don't know why I said that. Really, it was a very bad idea as I had just opened the door to a hell of a lot of trouble. I knew better. I should have just run like I had stolen something. At that moment, I saw my tía Malia's store. It was just around the corner. I could have run. I could have screamed but I was a Chapa. I was Rico Chapa's son. I was Jesus Benítez Chapa's grandson; fear was not an option and I was no coward. The Chicano emotions took over my spirit. I pushed my chest out like the rooster you're supposed to be and not a little, scared, white chicken. I had to show that I was man enough for what I had just signed up for out of sheer reaction. I brought my shoulders back and prepared myself for battle. Surely, I was a kid from Ohio but I wasn't sheltered like those typical, white kids. The Latino culture had taught me to confront my fears and to face it like a man. You don't chicken out. The cost of doing so is too expensive in the long run and will follow you forever.

During the times when my mother would take her long 'vacations', she left me and my brothers and sisters to fend for ourselves as she partied with one Casanova after another. I used to spend my time with my uncle Johnny and Pops at a popular bar. This bar called Latin Quarters happened to be owned by my uncle Johnny. It was full of go-go girls. Fights were a common occurrence. In fact, my uncle Johnny had been shot no less than five times in his own bar. I saw him beat many men to a pulp in the bar when they disrespected one of the go-go dancer girls.

"Uncle Johnny, what's the best way to fight?" I asked him one day

"*Mijo,* you've seen me fight many times before. Why ask?"

"What do you mean?" I persisted.

"Well, what did I just do, *carbrón?*" he said as if it was the most obvious thing in the world. And I had seen it. I knew it. I just had to apply it like a Chapa. I thought for a moment.

"Well, you kick the man in his private."

My uncle chuckled like it was the funniest thing he'd ever heard.

"That's right. I kicked him in his *chorizo*[27], *carbrón!*"

"Yes, I see."

"What happened to the man when I kicked him in the *chorizo?*" Johnny went on.

"He went down to the ground," I said as the logical response. My uncle laughed and gave me my first beer in acknowledgment of me catching on to life's realities.

But now I was in Texas alone next to an illegal immigrant whose last name I didn't even know and I was standing there telling him "I got your back." What the hell had just happened? Had I completely lost my mind getting involved in a stranger's fight? I had no business getting involved with this crap. My uncle Johnny was nowhere in sight to help me. I was getting myself into a mess that I could have easily avoided but that I somehow was drawn to. It

---

[27] Here meaning 'nuts'

was like my need to prove my worth, to be a man, and to show my machismo had come up in me.

At this moment, I didn't have a clear understanding of the consequences yet except that the one with the biggest balls would ultimately walk away the winner. Two of the guys came towards us as the other two stopped and watched. Everything seemed to happen in slow motion even though it all took place within maybe a few minutes.

My heart began pumping faster as the big, older kid came at me swinging a bat in my direction. I ducked quickly while David smashed the other boy in the face with his fist and broke his nose. I've always been a fast thinker and I react fast. It's like second nature to me and has proven to be quite beneficial numerous times in my life, and not just in a fight. This sudden fight, however, evolved so rapidly that it seemed you didn't even have the chance to count to ten. The kid went down like a bag of fallen tortilla chips. David's moves prompted me to kick the giant kid's chorizo as hard as I could with my skinny leg. Just like my Uncle Johnny said, 'down to the ground' he went. It was like David slaying Goliath and I felt about as powerful as a kid could. David looked at me in amazement.

"I got your back!" I told him. The two boys who were watching the fight started ran away fast after witnessing total annihilation of the guy in a split second.

"Another day, motherfuckers," they screamed out while their machismo vanished along with their fearful steps as they took off.

"You ever played soccer because you just made a hell of a goal!" David looked at me and asked me out of the blue in broken English.

The situation was funny. We smiled at each other and shook hands the Chicano way. From that bizarre and rapidly occurring event, I found out what it meant to be a real man; what it means to be macho. Being macho means don't waste your time with a bunch of chitchat. You get physical and take the first swing fast. You must show bravery and strength. This was part of what it meant to be Chicano; this is the strength of *La Raza*.

CHAPTER TEN

Cow's Head

David and I eventually became great friends while I stayed at my grandmother's house. Aunt Lilly used to tell me to work towards my goals. Her advice was invaluable and became one that I kept in the back of my head throughout my adult life.

I learned other lessons through experience, especially during the times I accompanied my aunt Lilly to work at King's Grainery. I lucked out and got myself a job at King's Grainery which gave me memorable experiences. While working this job, I made the acquaintance of a man named Joe. He was one of the hardest working people I've ever known. His job was to drive massive trucks of grain into the plant. He used to carry out tests by digging a metal pipe deep into the grain. I quickly picked up the technique from Joe. Soon I could do just the same and equally as efficient. The best part about this situation was that I could get my good friend David a job too.

It's interesting how we oftentimes get the most valuable experiences from seemingly insignificant situations. The time we spend with other people who has come to mean something special to you is invaluable.

David and I used to explore King's Grainery with great curiosity together. We were young and full of energy. As young men are by nature, we were adventurous as hell. After exploring the premises, David used to fly me around in his five-speed ride. He would cut corners and avoid death by a razor's edge. The adrenaline rushed through our veins as we raced like maniacs through the terrain. We felt immortal, invincible. The thrill of this was priceless for both of us. It was from those crazy rides with David that I learned how to drive a five speed. Those were incredible times when tomorrow seemed far away and our only concern was living life to the fullest right here, right now.

I remember the rich smell of grain that was processed at King's Grainery. The plant was more than just a job to me. It gave me a sense of pride. I realize that I could contribute to the local community through my work. I felt meaningful. It was yet another step in my development to become a real man and I was on a steady path to becoming a man through valuable lessons coming from all directions such as my aunt Lilly, my job, my friendship with David, and through the lessons learned from my very wise and loving grandma.

My self-esteem was gradually improving as I began to move away from the 'hillbilly'-culture I was taught during my younger years. The difference in the way Ohio men behaved and that of Texas men was huge and quite noticeable.

In Texas, it seemed as if the very concept of 'man' was redefined. You became a man at an earlier stage in your life. I was working now. I was surrounded by family love. Their love was straight from the *corazon*. This was a true love, a love that fulfills you, and a love that consumed the streets of Robstown where excited Chicanos blasted Tejano music day and night. This was the Robstown way of life defined by a unique culture, food, and music.

But above all, it was a culture characterized by love and family.

For a while during my time in Robstown, I went through a period of depression which lasted several months. Depression is a strange thing because you can seem happy on the outside and still smile but on the inside, you're tormented by despair, confusion, loneliness, and sadness. Sometimes you feel as if life has lost its meaning and you can't find your place. Nothing makes sense. You feel desolate and most of all just want to hide, get away.

My dad called me so many times and did his best to cheer me up with his Chicano enthusiasm. It's very difficult for outsiders to understand why you feel depressed especially when things seem to go in the right directions, as was the case for me in Robstown where I had the most loving and amazing people around me. I was making friends. My friendship with David was of a kind friendship I had never had before. We were even able to work together at King's Grainery. Of course, my dad missed his "little chicken." I missed my dad and I missed my brothers and sisters severely. It was very hard being separated from my family even though it was great to be away from the turmoil I used to experience pretty much daily.

Although I had no desire to go back to witnessing the alcoholic infused fights that my parents subscribed to, I still cared about everybody. I loved them and missed them. While away, I had built up my self-esteem through hard work. I felt stronger now. I had grown up. I had matured and I wasn't about to forfeit that just because I was dealing with a temporary bout of depression. My dad's attempts to cheer me up helped my depression some but it was the personal growth that I had undergone that really gave me the final kick. I had finally found acceptance. The veil that covered my Chicano roots had been lifted.

Sometimes people talk negatively about the cotton pickers and the fruit pickers. They belittle anyone working in agriculture in the heat of the burning sun sweating his or her ass off while slaving away for the white man to earn a shitty pay check. But these people are not nobodies. They're providing a job that many people wouldn't do because they feel it's beneath them. But let's face it. Without these workers doing the jobs nobody else wants to do, we would have a fundamental problem in society from the bottom of the totem pole to the top. They're part of my culture, my heritage, my life, and I'm proud to be part of them.

So how could I forget the outlandish stories the Chicano cotton pickers had passed down to me? Even talented artists such as Adan Hernandez, who I had to pleasure to meet while working on *Blood In Blood Out*, is just one of the many Robstown natives who came from this small town hardly anyone has ever heard of only to make a name for himself in the world of arts. Adan did an incredible job doing all the art work for that movie which was supposed to be the art created by the character Cruz played by Jesse Borrego.

Cotton pickers are unique people who stick together like a family. It's ironic how at one time even my grandfather had to slave away for the *gringo* by picking his cotton and now young Chicano kids were walking around with pride saying, 'Hey man, the cotton pickers are going to kick your ass in football' hinting to the toughness of the Chicanos.

Latinos have a knack for being able to turn something negative into something positive. They look at tough circumstances with optimistic eyes. They can turn the poor man's kitchen into a gourmet experience. They might find the fridge nearly empty with only a couple of onions, cheese, some tomatoes, a little tortilla and some cilantro left on the bottom shelf. The white man would think, 'Crap! There ain't nothing to eat in this damn fridge' and slam the door shut in frustration but to the Chicano it's a meal; It's the foundation of a delicious tortilla soup.

The ability to turn things around for the better is a very strong quality that Latinos have and I'm right up there with them. I've turned 'an empty' fridge into 'delicious tortilla soup' many a times in my life and I'll continue to do it reinventing myself continuously. That's the Latino way, the Chicano Way.

The time eventually came for me to leave my grandmother's house enriched by an abundance of memorable and great experiences. I had to leave even though God only knows I really didn't want to. I remember that night like it was yesterday. I couldn't sleep. I looked around the room where my grandma Juanita was sleeping and a tear fell from my eye. I was a concoction of mixed emotions that night as I waited nervously for that Greyhound bus to Ohio the next morning. I wanted so badly to stay but I missed my family too. It was a Catch 22. I decided to walk around the house quietly that night to soak in the feeling this home gave me. I wanted to take it in so to fix it to memory; the appearance, the smells, the ambiance, the details that so rapidly leave your mind, your recollection.

I walked downstairs and felt the presence of the house that felt like my real home. I slowly took in the photos of my dad and our Chicano family hanging on the walls. I checked out every little detail and stored it in my memory for good. I had mixed emotions as I took it all in walking through each room one step at a time. I felt sorrow but at the same time I also felt a sense of pride as I considered their souls through the pictures on the wall. You could see their struggle. You could see their suffering caused by all those years of blood, sweat and tears. It was written all over their faces. The evidence was found in their eyes and in the crow's feet edged around their eyes, something that only life's experiences and life's chores do to you. Despite the hardship visible in their faces, the main emotions that shined through the glass was their pride. No one could ever break their Chicano pride. These images have been ingrained into my mind forever, and I have turned to them for guidance during hard times.

I walked to another room and noticed a picture. In the picture was the table where all the Chapa's had at one time gathered with the great Chapa Patriarch, Jesus Chapa. The pride and respect the family had for each other was unrivaled. This picture represented everything my family stood for and its message stuck with me for the rest of my life.

I went outside and looked at the same place my grandfather killed a man who had disrespected his wife. I imagined the gunshots firing loudly. I could feel my grandfather's courage as I stood there pondering how he conquered fear. I took a deep breath and felt the pure machismo in my heart. It pounded like the force of hundreds of raging bulls.

As I stood there reminiscing, I recalled when I had first arrived in Robstown. I had been a confused boy. I had been a troubled and insecure boy. At the time, I didn't know who I was or where I was going. All I knew was that I had finally reached the Promised Land. The thick Texas grass really was greener on the other side.

I had seen a Mexican man with robust Indian features cutting the grass. He wore a cowboy hat and had a presence that is etched in my mind. He didn't speak much with my grandma. He stayed focused on finishing his work. He used to work in the hot sun as my grandma was making *migas*. She used to walk over with a glass of ice tea to offer him something cool to drink. It was in the exact spot where my grandfather shot a man in the heart decades before.

My dad spoke so passionately about his father, almost as if it was a fairytale. He used to grab a small glass of tequila before telling me a story that showed the courageousness of my grandfather. My dad used to pause momentarily to reminisce the past as he shook his head.

"Why did I ever leave Robstown?" he asked though not anticipating an answer from anyone. He spoke nostalgically of the people he grew up around and what they meant to him personally. He used to describe the way tortillas always laid in a glass holder with a towel covering them to lock in warmth but it was never just the food that defined the Robstown spirit; it was its people.

I will never forget the care they showed me and to this day I am still overwhelmed with gratitude for the experience, the chance to come to know true kindness and care. They accepted a white boy as one of their own and showed me what it truly means to be a Chicano. While I was standing outside, I remembered all the great events my time in Robstown had brought me.

Then I went back in inside the house and opened the fridge. I wanted some of grandma's leftover tacos.

Back then ovens were used for everything as microwaves had not yet become commonplace. As soon as I opened the fridge I let out a scream as loud as a four-year-old girl seeing a ghost!

"Ahhhhhh! *Abuela! Dios mio! Dios Mio!*" My whole body practically stiffened like that of a corps in postmortem rigor mortis status. My heart was racing from trepidation. I felt the little hairs on the back of my head stick up in alert. I screamed as if the Texas Chainsaw Massacre was chasing after me and my last sixty seconds of life was about to run out. What I saw in the fridge that night made me so afraid, so stinking scared.

My scream totally woke up the whole house. My aunt came running down the hall startled by the loudness of my scream. A million thoughts probably ran through her mind in a split second contemplating all the insane scenarios that could possibly make me scream like that. My Grandma slowly followed her wondering just the same: what on God's earth could be wrong.

"Damy! Damy! What is it?" they yelled at me. I looked at the fridge, my heart was pounding so fast that I thought it would explode in my chest any second now.

"Grandma, Grandma! There's a dead cow's head in the fridge!"

My aunt started to snicker while my grandma laughed without a pause for at least five minutes. I had never seen her laugh so hard in my entire life. Her Indian face shined bright like an Aztec princess as she sat down and grabbed onto my *guero* hand. She was laughing so hard that I felt the tears from her eyes drip down onto my hands. She then began to explain something that I had not learned about my Mexican American roots.

In Mexican tradition *Cabeza de Vaca* or "cow's head" is considered a delicacy, a feast of all feasts. The one thing my dad forgot to teach me about. To this day, I give you my Chicano word of honor that the cow was looking me dead in the eye and it was at that moment that I knew I had become a true Chicano.

CHAPTER ELEVEN

Redemption

I spent several months in Robstown embracing my Chicano roots. My grandma's Mexican tender loving care had caused my ulcer to nearly go away entirely. I had made great friendships, found a job and even found my good friend David a job. I felt blessed to have gotten the opportunity to spend time in Texas. It made me feel like a new Damian as if something inside of me had been revived. Regardless of how much I loved staying there, it was time to go back to Columbus, Ohio. It was time to go back to my family.

I rode the Greyhound bus on my trip back to Ohio. I reflected on all the things that had happened in recent months; what had led to my stay at my grandma's house, the events while staying at grandma's house, and what was awaiting me when I came back to Ohio. I felt as if I was in a state of limbo. You can say that in a way I felt like the song by the band Clash, a 'Should-I-stay-or-should-I-go-now'-state. On the one hand, I missed everybody terribly and I wanted to go back home. One the other hand, Columbus was the place where I had grown up and where my family was. No matter how wonderful my time in Robstown was and how it had helped my ulcer and changed me as a person, Columbus was my home. Because of that and despite all the shit that I endured and my siblings for that matter too, it was home and my dad was waiting for me there.

The other thing was that the big city was exciting to me. Robstown was such a small place, even though it had character like no other place, but in the long run the size was too small for me. I liked the city, the hustle and bustle. By nature, the opportunities in the big city were greater than it is in a small town, and my immediate family was there. The city life was part of the motivation for going back.

As I was sitting on the Greyhound bus, I suddenly realized who I was. I had changed, and in my mind, I had changed for the better. Now, I had a better sense of who I was, where I came from, and where I belonged. I had a much better sense of what my mission in life was even though I was still relatively young. The time I had spent away from Columbus had matured me. The little, shy boy inside of me was slipping away and I had slowly started down the road of becoming a young man.

I felt my mission was to go back and be a better big brother for my younger siblings. I also felt my mission was to be a better help for my dad as he always struggled with Donna Mañana in his life whether she was physically there or not. Let's face it, mentally she was never there but her physical presence made a difference regardless of the war that ravaged the house often.

I was not the only one who had suffered. Everyone in that house suffered, including my poor mother, but it was time for me to step it up and take on a man's role helping my dad provide for our family. It wasn't just my family; it was *our family*.

While in Robstown, I had gained a new understanding of what 'family' meant. I had started to see the grander perspective of things and how we're connected to one another. My Chicano family had taught me the meaning of family, of unity and care. Life in my Columbus home was often a living hell but it was now my job to try to make it better for everyone.

As I reflect on this today, I have come to realize the importance of forgiveness. It's truly the key to repairing any broken relationship even though we sometimes just flat out give up and choose to go our separate ways. It's not just in terms of relationships between men and women, between lovers, or between friends but also in terms of relationships between family relations whether it be between siblings or children or parents. Unless you try, everything is lost and only pain remains, even for the secondary victims of strife. Those who suffer the most is always the children.

When I came back from Robstown, I began to help my family more and I began to see us as a coherent unit rather than as a victim of a broken household, which is the perspective children often have when they experience similar family problems as I have.

The level of maturity I had reached in Robstown gave me a new set of glasses through which I now saw the world. As time passed and I became a fifteen-year-old young man, I eventually stepped into my dad's foot-steps and took on many of his functions. I put on a three-piece suit as did my older brother Rico. A portion of the money I began to make went back to my family. They needed my help. I applied the Chicano way to my life up north. I had learned a valuable lesson from what I had seen my Mexican family do. I wanted to make my dad proud of me and wanted him to see that I had embraced my Chicano roots.

I knew my dad had sent my grandma money from time to time. Up until this point, I had not realized why in terms of family values. It wasn't just about me becoming more independent. It was about helping my little sisters and my little brother too who continuously needed me.

I felt good about being able to take on that responsibility. It gave me a new sense of self-worth and pride. I felt stronger. I felt like a man now. I continued sending them money even after I took off for the big city of New York.

In the beginning of my career as an actor, I used to go back to New York City over the weekends but later I got a place in Brooklyn and eventually I got a place in Manhattan. I used to send them money and share my success even though I couldn't make it back to Columbus very often, or rather more and more seldom.

What used to bother me, however as the years progressed, was that when I eventually was suffering from tough times in my life, I didn't feel they supported me the way I had supported them. I resented it for the longest time. I felt they all forgot what I had done for them years ago, where were they when I needed them the most? Whatever the reason was for their limited support and whatever they were thinking, the fact of the matter remains that I felt abandoned and let down by them and that was the most difficult part of it. To suddenly realize that whose you love and have given so much to didn't have your back the same way when one day you find yourself fucked, that hurts!

Perhaps my Chicano blood just runs deeper than theirs. My siblings didn't go down with me to Robstown and maybe that made a difference. My mom was nowhere to be found. Whether she didn't give two shits about my misfortune or not, I really don't know for sure today. I hardly had any contact with her for decades but when you find yourself in serious times of trouble you still wish a mother had just enough love for her son to react one way or the other.

But it's water under the bridge now. I lost touch with pretty much all of them for many years while I had success as an actor in Hollywood and maybe they all resented me for that but in my mind blood should run deeper and you should be able to see beyond that when your family really needs you.

Man, did I need them suddenly but I was left with my sons and my loneliness. I have been through hell and back but despite it all I have no resentment toward my family today for all the terrible things that have happened. While struggling to make sense of life in recent years, I started to understand human beings more profoundly.

My faith in Jesus allowed me to understand more deeply what Jesus meant by 'forgive them for they know not what they do.' While I am a strong believer in that proverb, there are only very few people in my life that I resent beyond believe but not my family. Those who have caused me the worst hell in recent years I cannot forgive and forget but they are not amongst my family members. To make a long story short, I have forgiven my family and at the time when I was sitting on that long Greyhound ride all I wanted to do was go back to my family, as crazy as our family life was. They were still my family and I missed them terribly.

When I arrived, my mother is still not back but my father and my sisters and brothers were there. They had moved to a new house while I was absent.

271

That was not so strange because we typically moved every six to twelve months anyway. For us, to start over in a new home once again was just part of the norm.

We were like the Nomads in that respect. Every time my dad had rebuilt our lives and my mom was back, suddenly she would get a wild hair, snap and disappear for months and not ever call or write. At some point, she usually returned but the length of time varied greatly depending on what kind of crazy shit she was up to this time. Nonetheless, her taking off out of the blue caused continued hardship for all of us and we were constantly moving. It not only had an emotional price tag to it but certainly also a financial one. But in any event, it was not a strange thing that by the time I came back from Robstown we had moved once again. We lasted one time in the same place for about a year to a year and a half but that was unusual for us to stay in the same place for that long.

A few years after I came back I met my girlfriend Terri. At this point, my ulcers had pretty much disappeared. The lessons I had learned while staying with my grandma had changed me forever. My grandma and my aunt had given me my Chicano foundation which I took with me for the rest of my life. That's something that my mother, even if she had been around more consistently as a true mother, could never have given me although she did give me other lessons in life that aided to the construction of my personality and my professional self, which I'll get into later in this tale.

Upon returning from Robstown and forming a new life back in Ohio, I felt that with my ulcer that was reduced to next to nothing and I could finally live. I had a much clearer sense of myself and my life. I had found something in my life that I could be proud of and that gave value to my life.

I quit school when I was round 15-16 years old after I met Terri but not because of Terri but because I started working at my uncle Johnny's bar, the Go-Go Bar. I was managing the go-go girls. My work hours were long and at the same time I began working with my dad and my brother selling siding.

It was a crazy busy kind of life that I suddenly found myself in. I would work some nights for my uncle and then switch to days working for my dad. My dad was selling siding at the time and had started to do part-time bookmaking too but his core business was really selling siding. This was after his furniture business had completely gone belly up and he had to reinvent himself once again. My dad was like a chameleon in that respect, an artist in life transformations you may say because he did it so many times and it's probably from him that I've learned that skill too.

At this point, I was in my mid-teen years. I was round 15-16 years old and with my girlfriend. I hadn't seen my mom for several years or rather in about three years at this point. She had taken off but this time she had not returned like she usually would.

My girlfriend and I liked to go to nice places in Columbus, Ohio. Between my job working for my uncle and my job working for my dad, I was starting to make a little bit of money and life was looking good at the time. Although I was very young still, the money I was making gave me my independence and I quickly matured and became even more street-smart. With the life I had lived up until then, it had naturally caused me to become quite a street-smart kid. Additionally, I loved the financial independence that money brings to the equation. It simply amplified the good times.

I was a kid still but I was walking around in three piece suits feeling like a man. It wasn't until much later that I realized I really wasn't a man yet but at that point in my life, I felt like one. Later in life, I realized that I had just been a skinny kid feeling all cocky and full of self-esteem in his three-piece suit with a beautiful girlfriend, a wad of money in his pocket, and a gun in his waist line. I was hot stuff then and ready to take on the world.

Me with my hand on my gun ready to take on the world.

To a sixteen-year-old Chicano *vato* that magnifies his sense of machismo considerably. With money in my pocket and looking good, Terri took me into this nice restaurant called Gloria, if I remember the name right. As we entered the restaurant, I didn't expect to see anyone familiar. The place was packed with people. I was trying my best to be like my dad all dressed up and looking great in my suit. I had learned a lot from my uncles who all carried guns so naturally I thought I was the shit too.

Looking back, I was just a kid trying hard to be someone. I was learning from my gun-carrying uncles how to be 'a man' and so I too was walking around with a .357 Magnum. It was nuts because I was just a kid. I was not even legal yet and here I was in my three-piece suit and a gun feeling invincible.

Carrying a gun was part of the street life. It was just the way things were. It would have been strange had I not carried a gun. I had my girl and my gun in the holster and that was just the way life was. It wasn't because I had to look over my shoulder all the time and that I was getting into trouble. It was just for protection. And it was an image that I liked. Considering my family and the gambling I did here and there, it also just made sense.

With my mom's absence, she and I never made up after I came back from Robstown. There were periods when I didn't see her for like ten years even up until the end of her life. It never got any better. I left Columbus and would come back very sporadically. I came back when my brother was sick and I saw her but we never made up. We probably had max five encounters in the years after I came back from Robstown until she was on her deathbed but they were basically brief and superfluous encounters.

To make a long story short, Terri and I went into the restaurant and in the back of the restaurant there were two older and very handsome gentlemen with grey hair. By their appearance and posture, you could easily tell that they were wealthy. They had that stern and powerful look that doctors often have. I saw the back of the head of a woman with beautiful, I mean gorgeous, red hair. Her hair was all dolled up. She looked like a million dollars, like something taking straight out of a Federico Fellini movie. She was wearing a flattering silky suit which perfectly accentuated her figure and highlighted her femininity. She looked stunning to say the least. I only saw her at first from the back and at first didn't recognize who it was. She had an aura around her presence that few have.

"That's a really pretty lady," I said to Terri.

Terri turned and a look of shock came over her face.

"Oh, my God! That's your mother!"

"That's what?" I said in disbelief. "Oh, my God!"

My heart started to pound or maybe it even stopped for a moment. I couldn't believe it. I was truly shocked. I was thinking to myself, 'What the hell???'

At this point, I hadn't seen my mother for a very long time. I was very excited and my heart was racing. I was excited but nervous at the same time. I didn't know what to think. It was so surreal. Terri and I looked around.

"Let's just leave," Terri looks at me and says

Terri wasn't a big fan of my mother. She really didn't like her because she knew what kind of a mother my mom was. In Terri's opinion, my mother was the anti-thesis of a mother. She was everything that a mother should not be, and then some, and as painful as it is to admit, I would have to agree with Terri.

"No, no, no. Let's stay," I said as I started to walk back toward my mother.

My mother got up fast and she started to run back toward me. She looked fantastic. I mean she really looked great. To my great surprise, my mother started to talk to me in a thick Italian accent. I don't know where the hell that came from but it was kind of funny because she wasn't Italian nor had she ever to my knowledge done anything that would remotely make her pick up an Italian accent. She completely put on an act for whatever silly reason she had. She was so pretentious it was sometimes hard to figure out who she truly was. Her Italian accent was extremely thick but well done when she started to talk.

"Damy, Damy. Listen to me," she sounded like she was taken straight out of one of the Godfather movies. She the exaggerated way she pronounced the 'a' in my name and flattening the words.

"Listenahh... you are notta my sonna, okay'a." she said and she even added the broken English pronunciation to her Italian accent which is characteristic for Italian-American first generations to do. The situation was hilarious and very surreal. What the hell had gotten into her now? Only God knows. Her performance was priceless and very convincing. But it was clear that she was not trying to act funny. In fact, she was fully acting out the role of an Italian woman leading on two promising, wealthy men.

"Listen'a... Thosa two men'a... you have to listen to me. I wanna you to meet them but you are a... my... uhh... my cousin. Say you're my cousin or my friend or soneting".

She even rolled her r's like a true Italian would have done. It was flat out surreal. Had it been a painting it could have been done by Pablo Picasso or Salvador Dali. Her accent was perfect. She put on a great act.

I'm not kidding when I say she was like a character right out of a Fellini movie. Her hair was dolled up and she was wearing this sexy silky or satin outfit looking like a million dollars. She looked very young for her age so it wasn't too far off when she said I should act like I was her friend or something. At this point in her life, although she had been an alcoholic for years the alcohol had not yet affected her looks as it typically does at some point or another. The situation was priceless and I couldn't help but to laugh.

"You want me to tell them I'm your friend or something?" I asked her in disbelief. What the fuck was that all about?

"Yea… don't tell anyone you're my sonna. I told 'em I dun't have any. Just tell 'em you are my friend."

"Alright, alright. I'll play along," I comforted her.

Terri grabbed my hand and gave me stern look. She was not happy with what was going on and it was obvious that she wanted to leave and have nothing to do with my mom's crazy acting.

"No, you don't do that! That's horrible! This is not right. Let's go," Terri warned.

"No, no. I'm going to help her out. Let me go back there."

So, I went back and my mother continued with her Fellini act. She was practically Oscar Award worthy.

"Dis is uhh my friend'a Damian. Pleasa, say 'hello'. Dis is uhh Nicholas and dis is uhh..." she introduced. She introduced the other gentleman sitting at the table whom I cannot remember the name of. We were introduced and they were acting all cool saying 'Hey ya, how ya doin' Damy" like we're all pals.

These handsome guys had grey hair and were like doctors of something or other. If I remember correct one guy was in fact a doctor and the other was a pilot. We started to talk and soon I got a little too deep for my mother's comfort. She was obviously nervous that I would let the cat slip out of the bag and reveal the fact that I was her son. I'd be blowing her show that she was working so hard on and she clearly wasn't interested in the embarrassing moment when the truth comes out.

Scusi, scusi" she said addressing the two gentlemen.

She took me by the hand to lead me away and over to the other side of the restaurant. When we were far enough out of the two gentlemen's sight for them to hear what was being said, she turns to me.

"Okay look… it's uhh nice to see you but don't do anything. I'll give you a call. Give me your number," she said though in a rejecting way.

"No, no, no, it's okay. He's okay,' Terri rejected.

"Give me your number," I said and I wrote down my number and gave it to her but I didn't get hers. I walked out of there and I didn't see her again for like ten years or so.

After I got out of the restaurant with Terri, I got into the car and started to think to myself that it was amazing what a character my mom really was. She was all dressed up and playing her part. I thought, 'My God. She's such a beautiful woman'. But she was just a little girl that was hurt. Donna was just a little girl who had been messed with and that just wanted to have a life. My father had not been able to provide that life for her at the time. The life that we could give her was not what she wanted.

She wanted a dream. Now she was living the dream. She was hanging out with the high society guys; she was becoming 'La Dolce Vita". She was living that Italian dream that she had been searching for all her life; the escape from the reality she kept running from. Donna was creating a new reality for herself and was willing to lie her way to it just to gain what she so desperately was searching for. In a desperate attempt to create an alternate reality, she was even willing to lie about her own son denying my very existence even though I had been standing right next to her.

I was so disappointed and hurt. I could have been really upset with her. I could have been angry about the fact that she was denying that I was her blood. Instead, later as an actor, I realized I had learned something valuable from her.

I saw my mother before me and asked myself, 'How can I hate her?'

I don't want to hate her. She's a child underneath the cover. She doesn't know how to be a mother. She doesn't know how to love me but I must love her because no one else loved her. At that moment, I wanted to forgive her. I looked at her character and I realized that she was the reason that I became the movie star that I later became. The way she looked and the things she gave me, whether it was intentional or not, are all part of who I am today. She gave me the tools to become who I became so how could I possibly hate her for that? I'm sure she didn't intentionally do so but regardless of that, she really gave me what I needed to become Damian Chapa, the Actor.

I have realized that if it wasn't for my mother and father, however messed up their relationship was and whatever type of parents they were, there would be no Damian Chapa and there would be no Miklo. There would be no pain. There would be no suffering. There would be no emotions. There would be no laughter, no star success, and no real me. Without them, there would have been no emotions to be the artist that I am. I wouldn't have learned the art of acting, of putting on a show. I would not have been able to write the manuscripts I have later have written. I would not have been able to empathize with the characters I play and to become them the way I did with Miklo in *Blood In Blood Out* or the way I successfully played Bobby Fisher. Conclusively, it was meant to be. God works in mysterious way.

In retrospect, that has become apparent to me. Naturally, I didn't think of her in those terms as I walked out of the restaurant because at that time the Actor Damian Chapa and character Miklo had yet to be but it was meant to be. The redemption, I realized, was that who my mother was is what made me who I am. I am a strange combination of all the things that my mother and father were. As an artist, I have been able to draw on good and dark sides of them. All they gave me is a path. Because of that, I forgive her. It could also be that I forgave because it was the only way I could survive.

CHAPTER TWELVE

The Tin Man

In the next few years following my return from
Robstown, I went back to my dad and my siblings. I
went to work for my Uncle Johnny for some time
but eventually his bar was closed because he was
shot. This wasn't the first time that he was shot,
mind you. In fact, he was shot no less than five
times. The last time he was shot I came back from
New York to visit him in the hospital.

It was one hell of a scene at the hospital. It was
like something taken right out of the movie *The
Godfather*. There were two huge hillbillies standing
guard outside his hospital room for protection.
Uncle Johnny had survived getting shot once again
which to his gunmen was a real thorn in their side
as they wanted him cold.

But Uncle Johnny wasn't about to die so fast.
He was tough. This time he was shot in the head.
His gunmen obviously wanted to finish him off. It
wasn't meant to just scare him. The bullet, the one

that was meant to be the lethal one finishing the old Chapa boy off once and for all, bounced off his skull above his eye. This was the second shot to his head but it somehow ricocheted off the bone and he evaded death once again. It did cause temporary blindness but they failed to get rid of him.

When I entered his room, passing the guerillas outside, Uncle Johnny had a patch over his eyes so he couldn't see who it was that entered the premises.

"Who's there?" Uncle Johnny yelled immediately. Because he had just been shot, he was always on the edge. There was this guy Rocky in his room that helped my uncle. Rocky was a big, tall hillbilly who resembled John Homes the porn star.

"Hey Johnny," Rocky says to my uncle, "It's Damian. You wanna see Damian?"

My uncle nearly jumped up as much as he could, considering his condition.

"Damy, Damy!!! Let him in!" he yelled excitedly.

The gun-carrying guerillas outside, who were all puffed up and looking mighty scary to anyone who normally didn't hang out with my uncle's guys, moved aside to let me enter the hospital room. When I entered the room, I saw my uncle all screwed up from the attack. I felt sorry for him. He looked like shit all bandaged up and with patches covering his eyes.

"Hey, I'm so sorry," I started but he interrupted me instantly.

"Hey Damy," he said and continued, "I'm sorry I can't see you. Hey, man, do me a favor, will ya? Reach under my bed here. I lost it. I can't find it."

"Lost what, Uncle Johnny?" I asked wondering what that man was up to as he was pretty much as incapacitated as can be but obviously still mentally with it as he normally was.

"My gun! I can't find it. I put it underneath. I can't see nothing."

I looked underneath the bed and reached under in search for the gun to see if maybe it had dropped. I found the gun and gave it to him.

"*Chingao*, man!" he said as if a ton of weight just came of his shoulders. "I feel better now, *mijo*. Man, I'm telling you. If these motherfuckers come in here I'm going to fucking shoot them. It don't matter if I'm blind as a bat. I'm going to shoot 'em. Listen, if they come in here you just better duck real fast 'cuz I'm going to shoot 'em."

This was hilarious to me because the guy is practically wrapped up like a mummy in bandages and can't see shit but that is not going to stop him for a second from trying to blow his enemy away. He was unstoppable and didn't give a crap about anything so long as he was able to take vengeance. My uncle was a real piece of work in that respect.

"Hey Damy, my man," he says to me "I gotta close down the bar for a month or something 'cuz I gotta heal, you know. So, try to go get some work, okay."

At the time, I was trying to get work as an actor. That what I wanted to do. But basically, I was just trying to survive too. One thing led to another and I was just trying to make it. I got a hold of my dad. I didn't have a steady acting job in New York so I just had to do something to put money in my pocket while trying to get my foot in the door as an actor. I told my dad about my encounter at Gloria's with my mother. He asked if I got her number and I told him that she wouldn't give it to me. I told him I had given her my number but without her number there was no way of contacting her. I think he was sad, disappointed a little maybe. Truly, despite all the shit he had gone through with her over the years, I think he missed her. I felt bad for him. The whole situation was just sad on so many levels.

At this point in my life, I was going back and forth between New York and Columbus all the time. Oftentimes, I would spend my weekends in New York working my ass off trying to get an acting gig while during the week I would work in Columbus. This went on from when I was 15-16 years old until my late teens when I finally moved to New York and found a place in Brooklyn. Later, I moved to Manhattan and Lower East Side. While I was still living in Columbus and meeting up with my dad, he started to tell me about his new venture. This was after the awkward encounter with my wannabe-Italian mom. My dad had always been amazing at reinventing himself.

"Hey, look, Damy. I got a new thing going. I'm selling siding, *mijo,*" he says to me one day.

"Siding?" I asked wondering what my dad was up to now. "Siding? What the hell is siding?"

"You know, the thing you put on your house. That stuff that goes on the side of your house. It's called United States Steel Siding."

I was trying to figure out what he was up to now. He always had something going on. There was never a dull moment.

"Remember Eddie Braunberg?" my dad called me over to him. He gestured for me to come over like he had some genius secret plan that he wanted to discuss with me and he continued, "You know Eddie that I used to sell furniture with? Now, Eddie and I are in business together. He and I are selling United States Steel Siding, *mijo.* You're going to work with him. Both you and your brother Ricco are going to knock on people's doors." He carried on with his plan for a little while explaining a few details but not too much. Little information is oftentimes better than a lot of it.

The next step in the plan was the introduction to Eddie so I went to meet him at Denny's with my dad. He continued to explain how this whole deal was going to work.

"Now you and your brother are going to put on your nice suits and you're going to knock on people's doors. You guys are going to break the ice for Eddie so to speak."

He was a typical Jewish salesman with glasses and a very nice suit. He looked elegant and professional. Eddie was a trained actor in New York too and he would always approach me saying, 'Damon, how ya doin'?"

Eddie never pronounced my name right. He always called me Damon instead of Damian. Damy was only for my family. Eddie had a very thick New York accent and he was kind of loud when he spoke, not to mention full of self-confidence.

"Damon! Damon! I gotta tell ya. You're the first guy I'd wanna have as a what-ya-might-call-it? You're going to get us in house. Now listen, this is what the deal is. Me and your pops are going to bring ya guys there. Ya going to knock on their doors."

My dad chimed in supporting Eddie's game plan for how Ricco and I were going to play the game so to speak.

"Yea, Damy. You're going to hit the doors, like you're going to knock on every single door out there and here's what you say: 'Hello. My name is Robert. He continued explaining the script and instructed me to say but changing our names: "My name is Robert and I'm with United States Steel Siding and we're looking for a home for advertising. Mr. Braunberg has come all the way in from United States Steel Siding and we're looking for an advertising house to put siding on right there on the outside of your home. And aluminum foil insulation too." That was the introduction. Then he explained that they'll say something like, "Siding?

Oh, I like siding" because, as he explained, "a lot of these homes are made of wood." He was a gifted speaker too just like my dad.

On these woods built homes, the paint was coming off after some years of wear and tear and in Eddie and my dad's minds that gave us the 'in' with the prospects. We targeted specific homes that we knew from the look of the house were not the richest people in the world. They were people that would be looking for a deal and who would be easy to persuade and profit from.

Eddie and my dad knew exactly how to wheel and deal people. While the prospect was thinking that they were about to get a free face lift on their house, Eddie would spin it around and do his sales pitch.

My dad was the cool guy in the suit. My dad looked great in his suit while Eddie wore these Sears suits that half the time he had spilled mustard on. But even though Eddie's suit was messy he was an outstanding salesman. Eddie was the type of salesman that could sell sand in the Sahara Desert and ice cream to an Eskimo. He would not take 'no' for an answer. My dad would pump up Eddie as if he was the bomb. He would make Eddie look like he was the big shot factory man from the United States Steel Siding – whatever the heck that really was - and nobody back then would even think to question it as if it was the most normal think that the United States Steel Siding just shows up at your door step selling siding to any joe, jack, and jimmy. Using the United States in the name made it sound even more legit so any pinhead out there would automatically buy into it. People were more trusting then than they are today.

They were so good at what they did and so convincing in their sales pitch that no one even thought about questioning them. Truthfully, there was no Eddie from the United States Steel Siding. It was just Eddie the salesman. He ought to get an Oscar for his performance. That's how good he was. It was simply his whole persona, the sales pitch, and the acting he put on that made people swallow every word that came out of that man as if God himself had spoken. It would have been unnatural to question him. My dad had come up with the brilliant idea that Eddie was to represent someone of grand authority and it really was a genius idea to claim that Eddie had travelled a great distance just to meet this couple. It was a spectacular idea to make the customer feel selected and singled out. It won pretty much every single one of them all the time. There were very few exceptions. The game plan was a winner.

Rico, Eddie and Alex the Driver who always drove them.

To make a long story short, I would basically approach every single door in my target area freezing my ass off while my brother would target the other side of the street doing the exact same thing. We kept going tirelessly until someone responded. Eventually someone would agree to talk to the big factory man and instantaneously when someone accepted my dad would roll down that window and say, "come on Eddie" and the big, elaborate theater play would unfold.

They used to jump out of the back of the car and pull out all the samples of siding which made them look very legitimate. Once in the house, I would just sit back and watch the show. My dad's role was to open the show. He was the presenter of the Big Factory Man. My only role was to help pull out the samples. Otherwise my job was pretty much done and I would just sit back and observe the masters.

Eddie got the samples ready. They were solid steel.

"Here, folks. Look at this! Hit the side of it! Feel it!" he commanded offering the sample to the prospects to prove to them that they were the best quality. With his rough, blasting voice he sold them hard right from the get go.

"Folks, this is United States Steel Siding!"

He stressed every single syllable as if to reinforce the validity of his words. He sounded like the guy who introduces the boxers before the big fight with lots of enthusiasm and drama. The only line missing was when they say, "Get ready to rumble!" His lines were so well rehearsed that doubting him was unheard of. This was a place where his drama training came in handy.

The sales pitch went on for an hour. Eddie would go into details about the factory and how he had handpicked them coming all the way from the factory just to see them. He described the process of how they were going to put United States Steel Siding on all sides of the home showing the name on the side and how they were going to put new United States Steel insulation in.

He talked about how their house would look brand new after the facelift. The customer would get to choose color and they would discuss what would look best getting the couple increasingly interested. He always finished the presentation with an incredible show-stopper and never took 'no' for an answer.

"Alright folks!" He spread his hands apart while the rest of us sat back and listened intensely.

"Alright folks! I've been here for an hour and a half now. Now, Mr. and Mrs. Jones, I have come all the way out here from Pittsburg, Pennsylvania from the United States Steel Siding to bring you this siding straight from the factory. Now, I wanna discuss this now. If we put... let me tell you... if we install United States Steel aluminum foil insulation on your house and we put United States Steel siding on all four sides of your home and we put the insulation stuff underneath. The regular retail price is for this job WILL BE TWELVE THOUSAND NINE HUNDRED AND NINETY-NINE DOLLARS."

He nearly screamed the price like a circus manager presenting his most amazing circus act of the evening. Then he would do a dramatic pause like the great actor he was or like the dramatic, rhetorically rehearsed bullshit politicians pull that you've seen on TV all the time. Politicians sell their ideas like it is laundry detergent. Everybody in their right minds knows it's horse shit but they buy into it anyway.

And that is just what Eddie did too. He used rhetoric, persuasion and closing techniques to create a need for the product whether these people needed it or not. And he made them believe that they were singled out for this amazing offer.

"BUT!" Eddie screamed as he went on, "If you let me put a sign in front of you house for a whole month as an advertising house, and you let me take before and after pictures of your home, and you keep the price confidential," and then he would deliberately address the wife as if he was about to deliver top confidential government secrets to them and he would say, "Could you go close that window over there please? I don't want anybody to hear this." The funny thing is that the woman would always get up, and this happened every single time. She would walk over and close the window as if to protect them from being spied upon by outsiders.

The situation was hilarious. Eddie acted as if they were about to discuss top confidential military secrets right there in joe and jane's living room. I'm not sure how my dad and I really kept ourselves from laughing our asses off but I guess we were all just good actors. Eddie continued with his coarse voice.

"Thank you, ma'am. I don't want anybody hearing this. If you can do these three things. If we can take before and after pictures. If we can put a sign out for a month saying UNITED STATES STEEL SIDING. And if we can keep the price confidential." Another dramatic pause. Eddie let them sit and wait with great anticipation. It was all part of the act and it worked. Sometimes he would preach and sell so hard that he almost forgot to breathe while going through his show. His voice would become nearly raspy as he raised it like a TV preacher yelling out God's name while asking for donations. Eddie gave them his final, top confidential offer saying

"I will take THREE THOUSAND DOLLARS OFF THE REGULAR RETAIL PRICE of the job. THREE THOUSAND DOLLARS! And do the whole job, labor and materials for only NINE THOUSAND NINE HUNDRED AND NINETY-NINE! Hey folks, let me have your autograph right here."

For the most, Eddie would close the deal right then and there. He was amazing at his job. My dad quickly jumped up to get the paper work out and they would close the customers in the next few minutes. My dad acted all excited as if this called for celebration.

"Hey mom," he'd say, "Do you have some coffee? Or do you have some chicken? I need some good southern chicken," he would say showing excitement as if it was Christmas and we all just got the best Christmas present anyone could possibly ask for.

The papers were signed and next think I know we'd be eating chicken with them. This happen all the time. Ricco or I would get our foot in the door, my dad and Eddie would sell the hell out of them, and we'd all be eating chicken at the end of the deal. It was incredible. Money, fun and free food. Eddie and dad sold these nine-thousand-dollar jobs and we'd split the money. The cost was about $3,500. The profit was split between Eddie who would get two Grand, my dad got four thousand dollars and I would get like five hundred dollars so you can say we were like the camera search, Ricco and me.

For a young teen like me, it was a lot of money back then. If we told two or three jobs a week I had fifteen hundred dollars in my pocket. That was quite a bit of money for me back then. In my mind, I was basically rolling around in money. I had stacks of money in my pocket and felt like a king. I bought my own cars cash back then.

I decided at one point that all these characters that I had played in my life would serve me well. I decided it was time to do what I did best and that was acting. I had learned to act from watching my father and Eddie Braunberg and from watching my mother.

My mother was the greatest actor really. I knew what kind of actor my mom was when I met her at Gloria's and she approached me with that ridiculous Italian accent. She was outstanding. She was so convincing that you would never think that she was just a little girl from the Appalachian Mountains. Maybe it was her distant royal bloodline appearing from a distant past. Many families such as hers lost their crowns and money but my mother for sure did not lose the regal beauty. Even living years in hillbilly hell, she still had it. She acted her part so convincingly.

That is really where I learned my acting from. I owe it to my parents that I became the actor that I am. Even though I suffered from their messed-up household, the screaming, the fights, and even though the pain from my ulcer caused me to throw up blood on more than one occasion, I can honestly say that it's thanks to my parents that I gained the acting skills that eventually landed me the role of Miklo *Blood In Blood Out.*

After selling siding and everything else under the sun, my father became heavily involved with the mob. Later, he had many friends in New York and Youngstown, Ohio as well as Columbus, Ohio in that line of 'business'.

My father became someone the Feds wanted to capture but never could. He was not some wanna-be actor in a Scorsese film. He was the real thing. He used to go in and out of being a salesman as he tried to only deal with some of the biggest bookies on the East Coast. My father finally settled with the mob and found a decent job as one of the biggest bookies in Columbus. He did many things in addition to being a bookie, things that I care not to repeat.

However, the Feds tried to get Rico the Bookie but never did. He was too slick. My other uncles were caught all the time. One of my uncles was arrested for being a hitman and spent years in prison. That is a long story though.

But my dad became what he had to become to survive. He went through hell in life with mother and I know deep in his heart he wanted to be a good man. He wanted to be a respectable man in society just like my uncle Bobby had become. But for my dad, it was just like Michael in the Godfather film. He tries to stay straight but it just didn't happen because he had to survive too.

This thing happened with the Miklo character in *Blood In Blood Out* too. He wanted to straighten out but it just doesn't happen. He had to survive.

My dad died with a reputation of being a small-time gangster. He earned his respect undeniably. My father was known for pulling a pistol whenever need be. Him and my uncles were no one to fuck with. I went on to become an actor. I only played these types of characters that I knew well from personal experience. I grew up with the real thing. Both my father and mother probably tried in their own way to make things good. They just didn't have what it takes but that might have been what helped me later.

My poor mother. She was so beautiful but so torn. She was so regal but so scathed. Maybe they just didn't get a chance in life. Maybe they didn't have enough time to find out who they were and to find a way to be what they should have been. Maybe they just tried to survive what happened to them. I know my mother did some crazy thing but she gave me her features. These are the features that I guess made me the movie star I became for a while. Maybe she also gave me the eccentric personality traits that I have and which worked for me in arts and acting. I admit that it is hard to forgive but I also believe that somehow, somewhere the answer to why things were the way they were will be given to us. Why did I and so many others have to have dysfunctional parents and why do we have to suffer? Instead of focusing on the negative, I want to focus on the good things in life. Those crazy, hurt kids, that is my mother and father, gave me the gift I needed to get a lot of work as an actor and filmmaker. Because of that, I must be grateful.

IF MY MOM AND DAD WHERE HERE TODAY I WOULD SAY:

"THANK YOU, MOM, AND DAD! I FORGIVE YOU AND I LOVE YOU BOTH. I HOPE THAT YOU FORGIVE ME TOO. I WANT YOU TO KNOW THAT ALL YOU ECCENTRITIES HAVE GIVEN ME THE FOUNDATION TO WHO I AM."

With Love,
Damian Chapa

My grandpa Jesus

Made in the USA
Middletown, DE
02 April 2018